ACTIVATING YOUR HEALING ENERGIES --
PHYSICAL, MENTAL, SPIRITUAL

With the power and the knowledge,
you can heal yourself

Ed Leary

iUniverse, Inc.
Bloomington

Activating Your Healing Energies -- Physical, Mental, Spiritual
With the power and the knowledge, you can heal yourself

iUniverse books may be ordered through booksellers or by contacting:

iUniverse
1663 Liberty Drive
Bloomington, IN 47403
www.iuniverse.com
1-800-Authors (1-800-288-4677)

ISBN: 978-1-4620-0171-2 (sc)
ISBN: 978-1-4620-0172-9 (ebk)

Printed in the United States of America

iUniverse rev. date: 07/07/2011

Contents

CHAPTER ONE

Introduction - The Energy Spectrum

Whenever I have a problem to solve, I know that both the problem and the solution are constructed from energy. If I really thought about it, I would probably conclude that all of my problems while on this planet earth were created by human energies. This is especially true of our health. Whenever I look for a solution, I invariably begin with physical symptoms and arrive mostly at a physical solution.

I know that we all have energies that are not physical. We have energies of a higher vibration with varying polarities that manifest as thought, emotion, subconscious impressions, and even spiritual impressions. All of these energies are required to promote true holistic healing. The healing energies that I'm referring to don't merely suppress symptoms either, as the general populations seem to prefer. Healing energies must treat the whole person both physical and subtle so that healing can be more permanent and more satisfying. In order to accomplish this, however, a change of viewpoint, a change of attitude, or even a change in beliefs is often required.

In addition, no healing is possible without an understanding of the laws that govern the physical as well as the more subtle realms of mind and Spirit. Violation of these laws is the main reason that we get sick, suffer, and die. Therefore, those ancient barriers that our institutions have constructed between science, psychology and religion must come down. Then and only then will we understand what laws we violated that made us sick, and what we must do to get well.

We all know what happens when we violate physical laws. The Law of Gravity, for example; If we jump out of an aircraft without a parachute, we know that, unless we can fly, gravity will likely destroy the physical body. Even more important to our health are Newton's Third Law of Motion, and the law of The Conservation of Energy which are not only valid in our physical world, but equally valid in the more subtle worlds.

Newton's Third Law of Motion states that "For every action there is an equal and opposite reaction,"

The Conservation of Energy Law states that "Energy can be neither created nor destroyed, but can be transformed to another form."

These will be an important part of our discussion on healing.

As a thinking and intuitive spiritual being, I have a broad array of laws that govern the subtle parts of me. These are not necessarily the laws of religious institutions that grew out of the teachings of true Masters like Jesus, Abraham, Mohammed, Pythagoras, Zarathustra or Buddha, but these often are the teachings that these true Spiritual Masters actually taught.

Chapter Two

Our Struggle to Survive

Pollution

It is incredible how many issues we as humans must know about and deal with in order to maintain this vulnerable physical body. For the last 30 years pollution has been a major concern. Then, in about 1990 all of my suspicions were confirmed when Vice President Gore announced that over 300,000 of us die every year because of pollution (Today's statistics reveal closer to a million deaths). There is no part of our personal environment that is not polluted: our food, our water, our air, our prescriptions, and over-the-counter drugs. This also includes chemical pollution, electro-magnetic pollution, parasitic, fungal pollution, and food that our unique bodies cannot use.

Keeping Healthy

In spite of all the negativity surrounding us, there are things we can do as individuals to promote a healthy, relatively pain-free lifestyle. Therefore, I would like to share with you a few of the things I have learned over the past 30 years that have caused me to make my health the most important concern of my life.

When I was young, maintaining health of the physical body never entered my mind. As long as I felt good, why should I be concerned about my health? Once I entered my thirties, my reckless lifestyle and lack of concern for health took its toll. First it was Mononucleosis, Kidney stones, then neck and back pain. I was gaining weight. My clothes didn't fit me anymore. I must either loose weight or buy a new wardrobe. Since my budget was quite small in those days, I chose the former alternative.

Amazingly, loosing weight was not difficult for me. I'll share some techniques later in this book. My initial concern for my weight also forced me to place attention, for the first time in my life, on feeling good. Although I've never been concerned about living a long life, the quality of my life has been a major focus during my last 30 years. It has been a constant process of learning, adjusting my diet and trying new things.

National Health Care

One thing I've learned is the sad state of our national health care system. More and more of our citizens are beginning to realize that our family physicians do not heal. They diagnose an illness and prescribe a drug that may suppress the symptom temporarily. Discovery of the root cause is never a concern for the traditional MD (Medical Doctor). Nine times out of ten the drug will create new symptoms that must be suppressed by another drug. I once knew a lady who was taking 12 different expensive drugs at one point in her life. She still didn't feel that good most of the time. They call this health maintenance. I call it disease maintenance.

The Root Cause of Illness

A major focus of this book will be discovering the root cause of illness and attacking that. More often than not, the remedy will be a change of habit, diet, thinking, and lifestyle. For many people this will be difficult. I will also share some easy guidelines to follow in the area of self-discipline. Nothing has to be difficult once we decide that it's not going to be. Here are the "physical" keys:

Making Clean Energy

I remember an experiment from my high school physics class where we passed an electrical current through a beaker of water (H_2O) causing the Hydrogen atoms to be separated from the oxygen atoms resulting in the equation: $H_2O \rightarrow 2H_2 + O_2$ In this process, the energy of the electrical current is absorbed.

Today, many automobile companies are experimenting with Hydrogen as a fuel. When our auto is burning hydrogen as a fuel we have the opposite equation: $2H_2 + O_2 \rightarrow H_2O$. In this case energy is radiated within the automobile cylinder to drive the auto. Many environmentalists believe this to be the ideal nonpolluting fuel for automobiles. You construct large panels of solar cells in the desert to generate the electrical current needed to break down the water molecule into Hydrogen and Oxygen. This is collected and combined in the auto cylinder to produce nonpolluting energy and water. Don't look for this anytime soon as long as the oil barons have anything to say.

CHAPTER THREE

Breathing Clean Air

It was when I visited Florida several years ago that I became friends with the Naturopathic Doctor, Robert Morse, who currently has a detoxification clinic in Port Charlotte, Florida (www.GodsHerbs.com). Just before we parted I asked him: "if I were to read only one book on health, what would you recommend?" Without hesitation he answered *Man's Higher Consciousness* by Dr. Hilton Hotema.

Breatharianism

Dr. Hotema suggested that the most important thing we can do for our health is deep breathing in a clean air environment. He suggested that we can exist without food. His philosophy was that all the elements required for health are in the air. If you search the Internet for the word Breatharian, you will come up with organizations of people who eat little or no food. One such Web site is: www.breatharian.com.

Dr. Hotema actually suggests a program for a gradual transition leading to what he called breatharianism. Beginning as a meat eater, one can gradually give up meat and become a vegetarian eating only fruits and vegetables. Secondly, one would gradually give up vegetables and eat only fruits. Thirdly one would give up solid foods and become a liquidarian. Finally, they would give up even liquids and become a breatharian.

Needless to say this would not be easy. I've reached the liquidarian stage twice in my life and practiced it for 10 and 14 days. I did the fast merely to give the body time to purge itself of toxins that built up over a period of years. You will seldom if ever hear this from an MD, but toxins, not germs or viruses, are one root cause of illness.

Wiley Brooks, Breatharian, Spiritual Teacher, and writer was the founder of the Breatharian Institute of America. Wiley has been a Breatharian for some 30 years and has been giving seminars and teaching his intrinsically learned philosophy for over 20 of those years. A Breatharian is a person who can, under the correct conditions, live with or without eating food. Wiley first introduced the practice to the world back in 1981 when he appeared on the national TV show "THAT'S INCREDIBLE" demonstrating his strength by lifting 1100 lbs of weights, nearly 10 times his body weight. When in a non-polluted environment, (Air or Electro) he sleeps 1 to 7 hours a week. Although Wiley is over 66 years of age he is still able to lift 600 to 900 lbs of weight without ever working out. What Wiley did 30 years ago, would be much more difficult today, says Wiley who has found four major deterrents to being able to live totally without food today. They Are: People pollution, water pollution, food pollution, air pollution, and electromagnetic pollution

Living on Light

A lady by the name of Jasmuheen has written a book called *Living on Light* which implies that spiritual persons who have strong faith can live on spiritual light. Jesus and many saints have been pictured with a light around them. Occasionally, I am shown a photograph of a seemingly ordinary person with a light around them.

Occasionally, I will have experiences that reinforce my belief in the phenomenon. I noticed that when I am writing my articles and books, and the words are flowing fluidly, I can go a whole day or more without getting hungry or even thinking of food. Great scientists and artists have reported similar experiences. I believe that spiritual energy sustains the physical body of those in a state of creative upliftment. When I become weak while exercising, I imagine a beam of light coming through the top of my head and filling my whole body. This definitely gives me the energy to continue strenuous exercise.

Diminished Oxygen

Getting back to the importance of breathing clean air, it is every bit as important as any other factor, since without oxygen, we die. Our planet has less than half the oxygen in the air we breathe that we had 100 years ago. Thousands of acres of trees and forests are destroyed every year. Ninety percent of them are never replaced by the lumber companies that destroy them. Trees are a major source for oxygen. Burning fossil fuels, besides polluting the air, remove mass quantities of oxygen. As most of us are aware, our beautiful planet is in crisis trying to deal with our abuses.

Indoor Pollution

In spite of this high level of pollution in our outdoor environment, our indoor environment is much more polluted. Pollution inside of our homes has many sources: Bacteria from molds and mildew wherever moisture accumulates in the home, chemical fumes from all detergents and cleaners (unless you are using natural products like Miracle-II), air fresheners (can be highly toxic), paints, perfumes, and solvents, cigarette smoke (contains nearly 1000 chemicals), animal hair and dander, combustion of any fuel from your furnace, gas log or wood-burning fireplace, fumes from paints or solvents, and fumes from pesticides. There can be fumes from your furniture, carpets and even the building itself.

Political Activism

Besides petitioning Congress through organizations like save Our Environment (http://www.savingourenvironment.org/) things we can do to minimize the effects of air pollution on our health. I usually keep a lot of plants in my house that help considerably. Certain plants also help to remove pollution from the air like, Golden Pathos, Philodendron, and Spider Plants. Over the years I have used a variety of air purifiers as well. Many of our appliance stores have air purifiers. Some air purifiers generate ozone similar to the way an electric thunder storm does.

Electrical storms generate ozone when lightening strikes. The chemical symbol for ozone is O3, meaning it is made up of two stable oxygen atoms (O_2) with one extra, less stable atom. This extra atom will quickly break loose from the ozone molecule and become an ion of oxygen. This results in more oxygen (O_2) in the air plus air-cleaning ions that attach themselves to pollution particles making them harmless. I have been testing one of these units for several years now and have been quite impressed thus far.

The product I am testing is called Prozone. Prozone creates a process similar to that of Mother Nature when generating ozone. We all know what the air smells like after a thunderstorm. My rooms are beginning to smell similar to this since I've been using Prozone.

There is currently some controversy, however, about the effect of ozone when we breathe it. Robert B. Olcerst, Ph.D., CIH, DABT, CSP of Brujos Scientific Inc. - Industrial Hygiene and Toxicology, states that:

> Every chemical substance has a range of effects on biological systems that range from healthy to no effect, to levels of lethality. In effect, every chemical has the capacity to be toxic, and it is usually dosage that becomes significant. Ozone is no exception. At extremely high concentrations there are indications that ozone can be harmful. However, in the case of smog, studies show that ingredients other than ozone, the nitrogen oxides, sulfur oxides, suspended sulfuric acid, nitric acid particles and suspended hydrocarbons that are the real health risks.

> The important questions become: how much ozone is being generated by the air purifiers on the market, and how rapidly is ozone (O_3) breaking down into O and O_2? How rapidly this

occurs is affected by the amounts of ozone precursor chemicals, from the weather and climate factors, sunlight, warm temperatures, stagnant high-pressure weather systems, and low air circulation.

In a highly polluted environment Ozone can break down rapidly. If no pollutant is present, oxidation takes place within the ozone molecule itself (the third atom that makes the molecule unstable) causing the ozone to revert to pure oxygen within a period of 20 to 30 minutes (http:// www.inspiredliving.com/airpurifiers/ozone.htm

When I first purchased my Prozone unit I had it running 24 hours a day for months and never experienced any adverse health affect. I've also never heard of anyone experiencing health affects more serious than a headache or mild nausea. If this happens, I just turn off the unit for awhile.

We need oxygen because every cell in our body will die without it. A number of supplements on the market can also make oxygen available to our cells. This is another way of purifying your water as well as getting more oxygen to your cells. Miracle-II is such a product.

CHAPTER FOUR

Drinking Pure Water

Importance of Water

Several years ago, I attended a series of lectures by a doctor who used natural methods for healing illness. Her major focus was forming habits that will enable you to feel good all of the time. Before each lecture she would ask the audience: What's the most important ingredient in your diet? Because of her subsequent lectures, everyone knew to call out: Water!!! The most beneficial practice we can do for our health, she insisted, is to drink eight to ten (8 ounce) glasses of water every day. Besides being beneficial to overall health, it has also been known to keep the fat from accumulating in our bodies. It has been described as "the single most important catalyst in losing weight and keeping it off." When our stomach gets empty, we get that hungry feeling that we want to satisfy. To get rid of that feeling we fill our stomach with food, but water would fill it just as easily.

We all know how fresh and clean the air smells after a warm summer rain. We also feel much better after a good bath or shower. It's even more important to keep our internal vital organs washed clean. Our bodies know how to do this but only if it has enough water. This doesn't mean just any liquid either. It means pure clear water. Water is required to bring nutrients to the cells as well as to carry toxins and waste from the body. According to author and researcher Dr. Hulda Clark, the root cause of all illness is the buildup of toxins in joints or some major organ in the body, and/or the invasion of parasites. Without water it's impossible for the body to perform its natural functions of ridding the body of these invaders.

Here are a few facts about the benefits of water:

- One glass of water shuts down midnight hunger pangs for almost 100% of the dieters studied in a University study.
- The lack of water is the #1 trigger of daytime fatigue.
- Preliminary research indicates that 8-10 glasses of water a day could significantly ease back and joint pain for up to 80% of sufferers.
- A mere 2% drop in body water can trigger fuzzy short-term memory, trouble with basic math, and difficulty focusing on the computer screen.
- Drinking 5 glasses of water daily decreases the risk of colon cancer by 45%, slashes the risk of breast cancer by 79%, or reduce bladder cancer by 50%.

Finding Pure Water

This brings us to the second problem: finding a pure water source. Water from your kitchen tap is far from pure in most cities. More than 700 chemicals have been found in drinking water around the country, and the EPA has advised that 129 of these are a serious health risks. Interestingly, the EPA requires that municipalities test for only about 80% of these chemicals.

Consumer Reports conducted extensive research on the purity of water coming from different sources. The conclusion: city water is the least pure of any sources in the U.S. If you have well-water in the country your water is cleaner, but far from pure since pollution does eventually get to the water table. Bottled water is also taken from springs or wells and still contains pollution; plus the plastic containers can impart toxins to the water.

The Hazards - Some plastic bottles impart toxic chemicals to liquids that they contain. The National Resources Defense Council (http://www.nrdc.org/water/drinking/bw/bwinx.asp) has done an exemplary study on toxic water bottles. This table provides the best guidelines I have been able to find for providing guidelines on plastic bottle toxicity. All bottles I have examined have a triangle with a number on the bottom. The number indicates either OK or unsafe under the heading "Characteristics."

This table is provided by PLASTIC BOTTLES PTY LTD (http://www.plasticbottles.com.au/products.html

Fluoride - Here is an e-alert from the highly respected Health Sciences Institute:

November 13, 2003

Dear Reader,

It's fluoride time again.

The fluoridation of public water is a controversy I return to every few months, just to keep it on the burner, so to speak. This is an important health issue that affects virtually everyone who lives in or near any large population center in the U.S. And it's a subject that always prompts a surprised response from those who haven't yet heard that fluoride contains dangerous toxins, even though it's added to the water supplies in thousands of communities.

Fortunately there are ways to avoid fluoride intake. And believe it or not, avoiding fluoride just might make your teeth healthier.

Is there a way to remove fluoride buildup from your body? Good question, but difficult to answer.

Binding molecule - I recently received this e-mail from an HSI member named Owen:

> Fluoride is a toxin which accumulates in the bones and glands over a lifetime. It makes bones brittle, and has been linked to the plague of hip-fractures which effectively end the lives of 350,000 elderly Americans each year.

> I've been taking good care of myself for decades, but I drank tap water when I was a young man. There's bound to be fluoride in my bones, unless the clean living of the last 26 years has removed it.

> That's what I want to know:

> Are there foods or supplements which effectively remove fluoride from bones and glands?

Unfortunately, the answer to Owen's question appears to be, "No," so far, anyway. I asked HSI Panelist Allan Spreen, M.D., about the possibility of chelating fluoride accumulation from the body, and he pointed out that fluoride has an unusually strong binding molecule. This is part of the reason why many water filters are ineffective in extracting fluoride. Dr. Spreen says, "It's well known that fluoride is difficult to remove from water with conventional water filters. Much of the chlorine can be removed using a good carbon filter, but fluoride will not come with it."

I wish I had better news for Owen and all the rest of us who gulped unfiltered tap water for many years. Dr. Spreen told me he'll continue to review his research sources to try and find a natural way to chelate fluoride. In the meantime, this gives us an even greater incentive to avoid further fluoride intake.

Cumberland Blues - In a Daily Dose e-letter titled "Fighting Back Against Fluoride" (10/31/03), William Campbell Douglass II, M.D., featured the small town of Cumberland, Maryland, where the citizens adopted a charter provision in the 1960s to reject fluoridation of their water. But in 2000, a city referendum overruled the provision. Now that the tap water of Cumberland is fluoridated, many residents continue to fight the reversal of their charter provision in court.

In Dr. Douglass' typical, straightforward style, he gets to the heart of the fluoride debate with this barb: "But even if fluoride in the drinking water meant an absolute guarantee of never having to go the dentist again, EVER, you shouldn't consume it. Why? Because cavities can't kill you, but fluoride can."

Here's a quick rundown of a few of fluoride's potential dangers:

- A number of studies have linked fluoride to as many as 10,000 cancer deaths each year, with a high incidence of bone cancer among men exposed to fluoride.
- In animal trials, fluoride has been shown to enhance the brain's absorption of aluminum (the toxin shown to contribute to Alzheimer's disease)
- Several osteoporosis studies have associated hip fractures with fluoride intake

Add to all of this the irony that when too much fluoride is consumed, teeth can become discolored and crumble. How can you tell when you're getting too much? You can't! As Dr. Spreen stated in a previous fluoride e-Alert, "Whether you are pro or con in the fluoride controversy, there is one simple problem that nobody can dispute: You can't control the dose."

Land of the free - Usually when the government interferes with our healthcare choices, it's done by forbidding or restricting access. With fluoride it's the opposite; your freedom of choice is compromised when your local government puts a chemical in your water "for your own good." Every time you drink from a faucet, you're being medicated without your consent, or - in the case of the citizens of Cumberland, MD - against your expressed wishes. Want to hear some truly radical thinking? Many countries throughout the world have rejected water fluoridation programs based on the idea that health treatments should be a personal choice, not mandated by the government.

Meanwhile, tooth decay trends tracked by the World Health Organization from 1970 to the present show that the incidence of decayed, missing, or filled teeth has been steadily in decline with each passing year in the U.S., France, Germany, Japan, Italy, Sweden, Finland, Denmark, Norway, The Netherlands, Northern Ireland, Austria, Belgium, Portugal, Iceland, and Greece. Better oral hygiene and improved dentistry are the most likely reasons for this upswing in dental health. It certainly can't be attributed to the fluoride, because out of all of those countries, only one adds fluoride to the public water supply: the United States.

Water, water everywhere... - There are basically two ways to avoid the fluoride that comes out of your tap: You can drink bottled water, distilled water or find a reliable water filter that actually removes fluoride. That's easier said than done. To read more details about filters and bottled water, see the e-Alerts "Bad to the Bone" (4/29/03), and "Don't fill 'er Up" (2/13/03); both available on our web site at www.hsibalitmore.com.

Dr. Douglass has been one of the most outspoken voices in the fight against fluoride for decades. Recently, he consulted with a company to create a water filter specifically built to remove fluoride from your drinking water. For more information on the filter Dr. Douglass helped design, follow this link: http://www.agora-inc.com/reports/600SCTDF/W600DB98/home.cfm

When your local government offers a one-size-fits-all "medication" for the general public, just say NO according to Jenny Thompson of the Health Sciences Institute.

If you want to help change this practice of polluting your water, check out THE FLUORIDE ACTION NETWORK (http://www.fluorideACTION.net).

What are the Alternatives? - The *Consumer Reports* book also covers the effectiveness of water filters. The cheaper filters using only charcoal, remove some chemicals and sediment from the water but also leave some in the water. The claim of fluoride preventing cavities has not only been disproved, but fluoride has also been known to cause a broad variety of serious illness. Most filters do not remove fluoride from the water. (To obtain a copy of the *Consumer Reports* book, *Is Your Water Safe To Drink?* (Get a copy of *Consumer Reports* off your newsstand where you will find their address)

You can find a comparison of filters and distillers conducted by reliable AquaTechnology: (http://www.aquatechnology.net/system_comparisons.html).

Home-distilled water is one of the better choices for removing most or all pollutants. However, whenever the boiling temperature of a pollutant is the same as the boiling point of water, that pollutant may remain in the distilled water. The Waterwise Distiller with carbon filter (www.Waterwise.com) claims that their system does remove fluoride and most other pollutants.

Water filters - The cheaper, one-stage filters that you find in the discount houses will remove some of the pollutants but far from all. You may pay $100 or more for the better filters, but you know you have good water, which isn't the case with cheap filters or any of the bottled waters.

The filtering system that removes fluoride that I have used in the past is called the BEV Water System. It has a six stage filtering system including reverse osmosis and carbon filters. This system does the best job of any filtering system I have been able to find after having tried many systems over the last ten years. Unfortunately, you have to change the filters every year and this can be a real headache. (The BEV water System may be purchased from Plexus, publishers of the highly recommended book Young Again by John Thomas, 1-800-659-1882 or 1885).

CHAPTER FIVE

Finding Pure Food

When most people hear the words "healthy" diet they think about eating the foods that contain all of the nutrients required to maintain the body's health. This is only one aspect of diet. The second and most important aspect of diet is eating foods that have the least amount of toxins or elements your own unique body can't use and will end up impairing the functions of vital organs. The fewer elements you ingest that the body can't use and must flush out, the more energy the body will have to use for pain-free physical activity.

Unfortunately, most foods today make the body use more energy to process than is provided to the body by the food being ingested. Most processed foods that we ingest are seldom digested sufficiently enough to extract needed nutrients. The body spends all of its energy trying to break down solid foods, then getting rid of unneeded byproducts. Raw fruits seem to give me more energy than any other food. It is easily digested, plus it has its own enzymes to help with the process of digestion. As our bodies grow older, they no longer produce all of the enzymes needed for the digestion of the foods we eat.

Even more importantly, cooked foods provide little or no energy for the body to use for productive activities.

What are we putting into Our Bodies?

The general rule that we humans follow as we plod through life is: "Seek pleasure and avoid pain." With a little experience as an adult, however, we soon discover that this rule will often get us into trouble. I know a few of my friends would love to subsist on a diet of Big Macs, pizza and cokes. They give pleasure, yes, but they nearly always result in what we don't want, pain.

When I first met Dr. Robert Morse, ND, back in the 1980s he was advising all of his cancer and aides patients to "Eat Raw Food." If they followed his advice their bodies healed naturally without radiation, chemo, surgery, or drugs. In his recent seminar he repeatedly emphasized the point that dead (cooked) foods are devoid of energy, and whatever the body cannot benefit from, it must expend energy to reject.

I became curious about why I don't have more energy, and often fall asleep, after a cooked meal. Then I stumbled onto the Web site:

http://www.living-foods.com/articles/rawfreshproduce.html and the title *Raw Fresh Produce vs. Cooked* Food popped into view.

What does cooking do to Nutrients in Our Food?

When food is cooked above 117 degrees F for three minutes or longer, the following deleterious changes begin, and progressively cause increased nutritional damage as higher temperatures are applied over prolonged periods of time: 1. Proteins coagulate and high temperatures denature protein molecular structure, leading to deficiency of some essential amino acids, 2. Carbohydrates caramelize ("Caramelized Carbohydrates" are said to be carcinogenic), 3. Fats - overly heated fats generate numerous carcinogens including acrolein, nitrosamines, hydrocarbons, and benzopyrene (one of the most potent cancer-causing agents known), 4. Natural fibers break down, cellulose is completely changed from its natural condition: it looses its ability to sweep the alimentary canal clean, 5. Vitamins & Minerals - 30% to 50% of vitamins and minerals are destroyed, 6. Enzymes - 100% of enzymes are damaged and loose their effectiveness as catalysts for essential cellular functions. The body's enzyme potential is depleted which drains energy needed to maintain and repair tissue and organ systems, thereby shortening the life span, 7. Pesticides found in most foods are restructured into even more toxic compounds, 8. Valuable Oxygen is lost, 9. Destructive Free Radicals are produced, 10. Pathogens - cooked food pathogens enervate the immune system, 11. Nucleic Acids and Chlorophyll - heat degenerates nucleic acids and chlorophyll, 12. Inorganic Minerals - cooking causes inorganic mineral elements to enter the blood and circulate through the system which settle in the arteries and veins, causing arteries to lose their pliability. The body prematurely ages as this inorganic matter is also deposited in various joints or accumulates within internal organs, including the heart valves. As temperature rises, each of these damaging events reduces the availability of individual nutrients. Modern food processing, that usually requires high temperatures, not only strips away natural anti-cancer agents, but searing heat forms potent cancer-producing chemicals in the process. Alien food substances are created that the body cannot metabolize.

It may have been sufficient to say that cooking raw foods destroys the Life Force and changes their polarity from positive to negative. This is in direct opposition to promoting the health of the body, thus causing injury to cells rather than nourishing them. Raw, living foods still have their vital LIFE FORCE in them, dead, cooked foods have none.

I recently attended a seminar by Dr. Morse, The three things that he said that impressed me the most are as follows: 1. "There are no incurable diseases," 2. "The cells of our body cannot long survive in an acid environment" (a condition created by the typical American diet – cooked meat, potatoes and grains.) and 3. Medical Doctors cannot heal, Naturopathic Doctors cannot heal, Homeopathic Doctors cannot heal, Acupuncturists cannot heal, and Detoxification Specialists cannot heal. The cells of your body are the only true healers. All that these practitioners might do is to create a favorable energy environment so that each. A cell can do the job that its mission calls for: survival of the total being.

The Power & Intelligence of Our Cells

Every cell in our body is powerful and intelligent and knows the function of every other cell in the body. Once we create the proper environment, all the cells of the body will work together as a single intelligent unit. (This is extremely important to remember and will be expanded later in this book.)

Have you ever observed a colony of ants or a hive of bees? Each individual in those communities know their job as well as the mission of the entire community as a whole: survival of the community. This is precisely the mission of every cell in our bodies. They will work tirelessly toward the survival of the entire organism. You and I are the only ones that can stop them. We hinder them by what we put into and onto our bodies, and most importantly, by the mental/emotional energy that we have created with our thoughts.

pH Balance

Just as important as consuming foods with the spiritual LIFE FORCE in them is the effect that raw fruits and vegetables have on the acid/alkaline balance of the body. If the pH (acid/alkaline balance) of 7.0 or above can be maintained for a number of months, authorities say that the cells of the body will begin to expel toxins and pathogens and begin to regenerate and restore the youth of the human organism.

A product called Miracle-II Neutralizer (available through www.Miracle-II.com) has a very high alkalinity. I've estimated it to be around 9.0 on the acid/Alkaline scale where any pH below 7.0 is acid and above 7.0 is alkaline. Why is this important? Germs, virus, fungus, and parasites cannot survive in an alkaline environment. This is why I always add some Miracle-II Neutralizer whenever I drink water, juice, or a bowl of soup. After doing this for many years now, I began to wonder just how alkaline Miracle-II was making my water. I got a role of litmus paper and dipped it into 8 ounces of tap water. I discovered that water is highly acid and that it takes almost a half ounce of Miracle-II Neutralizer to bring the alkalinity over 7.0.

Eating habits

Many naturopathic dieticians insist that 80% of the digestive process takes place in the mouth. In order for the body to digest food properly, they say, it must receive the food in a liquefied form. This is seldom possible without sufficient chewing. Occasionally, I will watch patrons in a restaurant to see how many times they chew a steak or other solid. The count seldom goes over 10 chews. Is steak, or any other solid food, liquefied after 10 chews? Probably not. That body is probably getting little or no health benefit from its food.

Fasting

I am absolutely convinced that, if given half a chance, the body will heal itself. It doesn't even need our help. All we must do is get out of its way. This means stop putting all of that toxic food into our bodies. Have you noticed that your pets refuse to eat when they are ill? Did your parents force you to eat when you were ill as a child? "You must eat to keep up your strength is the usual reply."

If I have a chronic or serious physical problem, the best way I know to assure a recovery is through fast or abstinence. There are a broad variety of approaches to reducing food intake.

A. A total fast or total abstinence except water for as long as it takes.
B. A juice fast taking only juices for 10 days or more.
C. The Apple vinegar and honey fast.
D. The Lemon juice fast with maple syrup and cayenne pepper (called The Master Cleanse).
E. A fruit fast eating only fresh fruit and raw nuts for 10 days or more.

If I have chronic pain that won't go away, I do one of the above fasts for as long as it takes to get rid of the problem. The cells in my body have never failed me. I have done the Master Cleanse for as long as two weeks at a time.

Food & Nutrients

Do the foods that we eat have sufficient nutrients to supply the body with what it needs? Rodale, the leading advocate of organic gardening, has conducted extensive research into the nutrients in today's foods as compared to 50 years ago before commercial farming was introduced using chemical fertilizers, pesticides, and herbicides. Rodale has found that modern commercial farming methods produce food that is grown in soils that are toxic and severely deficient in the trace elements needed for healthy plants. When the vital trace elements such as copper, boron, iron, manganese, and zinc are absent from the soil, the plants grown in such soil will be deficient in nutrients. Modern commercial methods use chemical fertilizers that usually replace only Nitrogen, Potash and Phosphorous. (http://www.rodaleinstitute.org/)

Organic farming methods usually do replace the trace elements in the soil through various composting methods or using organic fertilizers. Rodale has shown that organic foods do contain many of the nutrients that are absent in commercial produce. Many of the smaller commercial farms are beginning to use organic methods because of the growing demand and the higher financial return. The added benefit of organic produce is: little or no pollution. Organic produce is the recommended alternative to supplements.

Since many of us do not have easy access to organic produce or cannot afford to pay the extra cost, we can use quality supplements extracted from organic foods. Supplements produced in a laboratory often cannot be used by the body and in some cases can actually be harmful. A good supplement produced from whole foods is highly advisable. I prefer a liquid supplement because it is easily absorbed by the body and easier to take. I myself use a product called IntraMax. It tastes good, has 100% Organic MicroComplexes, 100% or more of the 10 essential vitamins and 10 essential minerals, 28 essential amino acids, 10 digestive enzymes, 72+ plant-derived trace minerals, 9 pro-biotics, essential fatty acids (3.6.9), 25 herbs, 10 vegetables, 11 fruits, oxygen, and antioxidants. It's qualities

23

include, it is energizing, anti-aging, and an immune booster; it prevents colds, flu, and allergies; it improves memory, detoxifies toxins and heavy metals; it improves skin, blood, and bones. It is antiviral, antibacterial, antifungal, and antiparasitic. It provides the optimum daily allowance of all essential nutrients and more. Contact: Futeck.com, P.O. Box 6071, Sun City Center, FL 33573, 813-383-7594.

CHAPTER SIX

Loving Our Cells

The Building Blocks of Life

When selecting a beginning for a universal study, the most basic unit of life at the most mundane level would seem appropriate, which in this case, is the atom. We know that our bodies are a complex structure of different kinds of atoms often bonded together with other atoms to form molecules. 98% of our bodies are constructed from these six basic forms of life: carbon (C), hydrogen (H), oxygen (O), nitrogen (N), sulfur (S) and phosphorus (P). Like humans, each of these atoms vibrates at a specific frequency and amplitude (energy).

Molecules - These basic elements are combined in the body to form four basic types of molecules: lipids (CH, fats, oils, and waxes), carbohydrates (CHO, the energy-carrying compounds), proteins (CHONS, make up living matter structures.), and nucleic acids (CHONSP, hold the codes for life or DNA).

Water (H_2O) makes up about 60 percent of your body weight and is involved in almost every process that takes place. Water is the medium for the chemicals of life. For instance, we know that glucose is the basic fuel for living processes; however, it is only usable when it is in a soluble state or in water. Therefore, drink plenty of water.

(www.treedictionary.com/DICT2003/index.html)

The Cell is the unit of which all plants and animals are composed. The cell is the smallest unit in the living organism that is capable of integrating the essential life processes. In higher organisms like the human body, a division of labor has evolved in which groups of cells have differentiated into specialized tissues which in turn are grouped into organs and organ systems.

All cells share a number of common functions that run directly parallel to those performed by the physical body:

- Government or control of bodily functions is the responsibility of our Endocrine System, while Nucleic Acids in the form of DNA (Deoxynucleic Acid) and RNA (Ribonucleic acid) control cellular functions and heredity;
- Structure & Protection of the body is accomplished by the skeletal system, while cells use proteins as their main structural material;
- Digestion in the body is performed by the alimentary Canal, while cells synthesize proteins in the cell's ribosomes (ribonucleoprotein particles) by using the information encoded in the DNA and mobilized by means of RNA;
- Circulation in the body is accomplished by the circulatory system, while cells use the molecule adenosine triphosphate (ATP) as the means of distributing energy for the cell's internal processes.
- Absorption & Elimination in the body is accomplished by the alimentary canal, the kidneys and the skin, while the cells are enclosed by a cell membrane, composed of proteins and a double layer of lipid molecules, that control the flow of materials into and out of the cell.
- Inter-Cellular Fluids - All cells are surrounded by fluids that supply oxygen and nutrients and eliminate toxins. Blood Capillaries carry oxygen and nutrients to all cells and carry CO_2 for elimination through the

lungs. The Lymphatic System acts as a secondary circulatory system. Unlike the circulatory system, the lymphatic system is not closed and has no central pump. The lymph moves slowly and under low pressure due mostly to the milking action of skeletal muscles. Rhythmic contraction of the vessel walls may also help draw fluid into the lymphatic capillaries. Lymph nodes act as filters, with an internal honeycomb of connective tissue filled with lymphocytes that collect and destroy bacteria and viruses. When the body is fighting an infection, these lymphocytes multiply rapidly and produce a characteristic swelling of the lymph nodes. Many health problems begin in the lymph nodes. (http://en.wikipedia.org/wiki/Lymph_node).

Cells are designed to thrive and survive when their inter-cellular fluids provide an alkaline environment that has a pH of between 7.0 and 8.0 (pH is a logarithmic measure of hydrogen ion concentration in a specific food) and an abundance of usable high energy elements. Basically, these are the same elements from which the cells are constructed: carbon (C), hydrogen (H), oxygen (O), nitrogen (N), sulfur (S) and phosphorus (P). These should be contained in the foods we eat.

Foods that Our Cells Love Most
Cells love foods in the following order: 1. Raw Fruits, 2. Raw Vegetables, 3. Sprouted Beans, Grains and Seeds, 4. Raw Nuts and seeds, 5. Raw Eggs, 6. Unpasteurized Dairy, 7. Raw Fish, 8. Raw meats.

Foods that Our Cells Love Least
Foods cells least love in the following order: 1: Cooked Meats, 2. Cooked Fish, 3. Pasteurized Dairy, 4. Baked or Cooked Flour or Grain, 5. Cooked Eggs, 6. Roasted Nuts & Seeds, 7. Cooked Vegetables,
8. Cooked Fruits.

Why Our Cells Love Raw Fruits

Fruits create an alkaline condition in the fluids in which our cells love to be immersed. Your cells cannot use proteins, carbohydrates and fatty acids as found in plant and animal foods It is easy for your digestive system to break down fruits into the basic building blocks required for building and repairing the cells of the body: carbon (C), hydrogen (H), oxygen (O), nitrogen (N), sulfur (S) and phosphorus (P). Living foods also have high vitality that energizes the cells of the body. Living foods deposit these high energy elements into the surrounding fluids of the body for easy absorption by our cells.

Why Your Cells Don't Like Cooked Foods

Cooked foods that are high in protein and carbohydrates create an acid condition in the body's fluids in which your cells hate to be immersed. Our cells cannot maintain a healthy body for long while living in an acid environment. Also, our cells cannot use proteins, carbohydrates and fatty acids as they are found in the foods we eat. It is not easy for your digestive system to break down meats and grains into the basic building blocks during the 6 to 10 hours that they remain in the digestive tract.

It is my opinion that elements in many foods such as meats, cheeses, fish, grains, nuts, seeds, and hard vegetables are not in the body long enough to be transformed into the only elements that the body can use: carbon (C), hydrogen (H), oxygen (O), nitrogen (N), sulfur (S) and phosphorus (P). In fact, a study by Dr Hilton Hotema showed that the body never absorbs any of the food taken into the body. I am convinced that the only benefit that our cells get from food is from the frequency and energy of the vibrating elements (atoms) in living foods. Cooked foods provide our cells with zero energy. In fact cooking turns many food nutrients into elements that are toxic to our cells. If I boil my body, I die.

Energy

Where does the body's energy come from? Many would say from food, or the sun. Followers of a philosophy called

Breatharianism, who eat little or no food, would say they get their energy from the air. Jasmuheen, in her book *Living on Light*, says, "...the force that drives the human machine is not chemical but Etheric." While taking occasional teas for enjoyment, she insists that she has been physically nourished by the Universal Life Force she calls Prana and what others call Chi, orgone, Eck, or the Holy Spirit.

Physicists have shown that a single atom has incredible energy. David Bohm, a University of London physicist and protégé' of Albert Einstein, after observing the behavior of atoms for decades, insists that every atom has the energy and the intelligence of the whole which seems to imply what most religions believe - that God is everywhere.

The Fear Factor

We have all experienced "the fear factor" when we encounter frightening situations in life. None are more fearful than the life-threatening pronouncement of a trusted physician; you have the big "C!" I'm convinced that it is not cancer, heart disease or stroke that kills us, but rather the fear that grips us after our doctor gives us his judgment. Doctors don't know everything, particularly the omniscience and omnipotence of every atom in our body.

Love Conquers All

Whenever that fear grips my heart, I go within myself, focus my attention on the Heart Center, and sing HU silently or aloud. I call this my "Love Song to God." I sing it until the fear is dissolved. If it comes back later, I repeat the exercise. There is no emotion, thought, or challenge in life that cannot be resolved with this exercise. Jesus said it this way: "Seek ye first the kingdom of God and all of these things will be given you besides."

Exercise

The second most important thing you can do for the physical wellbeing of our cells is exercise, and it doesn't have to be strenuous or time consuming. I spend about five minutes at a time, three times a day. I feel three types of exercise are important for a well rounded program, and the total program requires only 15 minutes a day total.

Stress is a major cause of illness. At the end of my workday, every muscle in my body is tense quite often to the point of exhaustion. One of the most important exercises I do takes place immediately after work. Stretching those tense muscles is the quickest way to reduce their stress. I do a modified form of Yoga, and then I lay down for a few minutes. I may drift off and sleep for a brief period, but mostly, once I've done the exercises, I'm no longer tired. I only spend five minutes on this exercise.

An exercise that is equally important is a form of aerobics. The up and down motion of the body places gentle pressure on every organ in the body. The action and the gentle pressure also acts as a pump for the Lymph system. The heart is a pump that brings nutrients to the cells and carries away toxins. The lungs pump oxygen to the cells and remove Carbon-dioxide. The cells deposit accumulated toxins into a network called the Lymph system. The Lymph system has no pump. The only way the Lymph system can remove toxins is through proper movements of the physical body. If this is not done toxins accumulate in joints, muscles, and even vital organs. According to Dr, Robert Morse (www.GodsHerbs.com), internationally acclaimed detoxification specialist, if you can remove all toxic chemicals and maintain an alkaline pH, the body will heal itself. Dr. Morse also insists that there are no incurable diseases.

Brisk walking, jogging, aerobics and rebounding (bouncing on a trampoline) are some of the best methods for pumping the Lymph system. I prefer the rebounding because of the potential damage to the leg joints on impact with a sidewalk or floor.

Exercise Makes You Smarter

"A study has shown that regular physical activity can spur the production of neurons in the memory region of a mouse's brain. One result was that mice who exercised on a running wheel learned new tasks better than mice who remained sedentary.

Researchers compared groups of old mice (about age 70 in human years) and young mice (age 20 in human years) allowed to exercise on a treadmill as long as they wanted with a control group that didn't exercise for a month, then gave all of them memory tests (finding a platform sitting in a small pool of water).

Older mice that exercised performed just as well on the memory test as younger ones did. Older mice that didn't exercise failed to remember where the platform was sitting, probably because they produced few new brain cells; scientists found regular physical activity spurred the growth of neurons.

This led them to believe exercise could hold the same promise for seniors in boosting their brainpower and slowing the forgetfulness and confusion that accompanies aging. The study may also suggest that people with diseases such as Alzheimer's could be able to build replacement brain cells by engaging in daily workouts. While previous research has demonstrated that exercise can spur the formation of brain cells in young mice, this is the first study that shows exercise helps older mice in the same way. (*USA Today_* September 21, 2005)

Chapter Seven

Electro-Magnetic Environment

Every function of our bodies, from heartbeat to motor skills, is dependent upon very subtle electrical signals from the brain. I am convinced that these very subtle signals are being disrupted by all forms of electromagnetic transmissions for radio, television, microwave, cell phone, wireless phone, etc.

Can Energy be Harmful?

"There's a gun pointed at your head," read the advertisement in the *New Age Journal*. How could I resist an ad like that? I continued reading and I learned that the gun they were talking about was the Electron Gun that shoots electrons at the phosphorescent screen of TVs and computer monitors. The problem: the electrons don't stop at the screen, but rather continue to accelerate toward our heads.

Now, I know the cause of my headaches, my burning eyes, my extreme fatigue, my lack of concentration, and my high error rate at the end of my workday. I sit in front of a computer screen for eight hours at my workplace. Then I come home and sit in front of my TV for another three. By the time I climb into bed I feel like a herd of elephants had just stampeded over my head.

I bought the devices that the *New Age Journal* ad was selling for $120, but after several weeks of use, the symptoms at the end of the day were still present. Now this situation really began to worry me. I made up my mind to get to the bottom of this, so I began some intense research.

My first step was to open a few books including my reference materials to see if I could find anything on radiation and CRTs (Cathode Ray Tubes) that seem to be at the root of the problem. Here's what I found.

What is Radiation?

Since those electrons shooting at me are considered radiation, I decided to start there. According to Webster, Radiation is the process whereby energy, in the form of particles or rays (such as light, heat, microwaves, etc.), is propelled or radiated into a space. This kind of radiation takes place at the atomic level and may be, for the purpose of illustration, viewed as being similar to our own solar system on a microcosmic scale. At the center of the atom (like our sun) is the nucleus consisting of protons with a positive charge and neutrons that are neutral. Rotating around the nucleus (like our planets) are electrons with a negative charge. When two atoms come into contact with each other, changes will inevitably take place. Depending on the nature of each atom: electron bonds can be formed to create molecules. Energy can be absorbed, or electron bonds can be broken causing energy to be radiated (thus the term radiation).

This radiated energy is of a vibratory nature and is commonly represented graphically with common sine curve and arithmetically with the trigonometric sine function. This curve represents the two components of vibratory radiation - wavelength and amplitude. A third component, frequency, is represented by the number of cycles that occur in one second. A fourth component could be the velocity of a particle or packet of energy radiated from an atom. The electricity coming into our homes has a frequency of 60 cycles per second, a voltage of 110v and 220v, and on the average 100 amps (Amplitude).

The most important components for our purposes are frequency and wavelength. These components are intimately related in the sense that higher frequency radiation always has a short wavelength and lower frequency radiation has a longer wavelength. Table 1 represents the broad spectrum of radiations that many of us are familiar (The values in the following tables are approximated).

Frequency (Cycles/Sec) Type of Radiation
$3x10^{13}$ to $3x10^{15}$ Gamma Radiation Short Wave Radiation
$3x10^9$ to $3x10^{15}$ X-Rays
$3x10^9$ to $3x10^{12}$ Ultra-Violet Radiation
$3x10^7$ to $3x10^9$ Visible light
$3x10^5$ to $3x10^9$ Infra-red Radiation
$3x10^5$ to $3x10^8$ Radiation as Heat
$3x10^2$ to $3x10^5$ Microwave Radiation
15 to $2x10^4$ Audible Sound
$3x10^{-4}$ to $3x10^5$ Radio Frequencies Long Wave Radiation

What is harmful radiation?

There are three kinds of radiation that can be harmful:

1. Ionizing radiation - Ionization takes place when an atom looses one or more of its particles through the application of heat, chemical action or electrical discharge. Such action can result in ionizing radiation capable of emitting high energy, alpha or beta particles as well as gamma rays and x-rays. Such radiation can result from atomic blasts and nuclear plant leaks. While such radiation can be extremely hazardous in high concentrations, the average citizen is not usually so exposed, according to official sources.

2. Electromagnetic Low Frequency (ELF) radiation - The most hazardous ELF radiation that the average household residents are exposed to come from your television and computer screens. The major source is the Cathode Ray Tube. This tube accelerates electrons at the rate of 2,600,000,000,000,000 meters per second. They pass through the screen at a velocity of 2,600.000,000 meters per second. Anyone that is closer than six feet away from the screen is at serious risk.

Other hazardous sources include: Television and radio transmissions, High tension wiring, microwave ovens, electric

34

blankets, electric waterbeds, fluorescent lighting, small electrical appliances, electrical transformers and terminals, stereo systems, incandescent lamps, wall switches and outlets, small bedside clocks, or anywhere electrical current is flowing. While one of these low radiation sources may not be hazardous of themselves, the accumulation of several could pose potential health risks.

3. Electric radiation - Electric current passing through any wire produces an electric field that surrounds the wire. The intensity and the size of the field depend on the strength of the electrical current. Whenever conducting objects – you and I can be considered conducting objects -- find themselves within an electric field, electrical currents are induced within those conducting objects - that's us. The induced current will vary according to the field strength, its frequency, the size and shape of the object and the object to ground resistance. Electricity that produces harmful electric radiation must be of a fairly high voltage. The average household normally does not have such voltage. An object must also be grounded in order to be affected by electric radiation.

Affects of Electronic Pollution

On March 8, 1990, Richard J. Guimond, Director, Office of Radiation Programs, U. S. Environmental Protection Agency began his report to the Subcommittee on Oversight and Investigations, U. S. House of Representatives:

> It is a pleasure to be here today to discuss the EPA's efforts in the area of non-ionizing radiation (Non-ionizing radiation includes emissions from televisions, computer displays, microwave ovens, household appliances, as well as radio and TV transmissions, and high power lines, etc.)... Historically, most of the available data on non-ionizing radiation primarily indicate acute health damage from short-term exposures rather than chronic health effects due to long-term exposures. Only recently has a substantial amount of data become available on the potential

carcinogenicity associated with exposure to non-ionizing radiation.

A few months later on July 25, 1990, William H. Farland, Ph.D., Director, Office of Health and Environmental Assessment, Environmental Protection Agency, was called before the Congressional Subcommittee on Natural Agricultural Resources and Environment (U.S. House of Representatives). The purpose of the hearing was to inform congress of the "potential health effects of electromagnetic radiation (EMR)."

"The Initial emphasis," he said, "addressed radiofrequency (RF) radiation. Radiofrequency or RF radiation is emitted from sources such as radio and TV broadcast transmitters, radar systems, and various communication technologies... Although we focused chiefly on RF radiation, some effort was also devoted to extremely low frequency (ELF) radiation, including the electromagnetic fields (EMF) that are associated with sources such as power lines and electrical appliances."

The kind of EMF radiation that Mr. Farland is referring to is radiation that results from a flow of electricity through a medium, such as the wiring in your housing and appliances. Certain appliances, such as your television, your computer, electric blankets and water beds, fluorescent, lighting and microwave ovens are known to emit higher EMF radiation than most others.

Mr. Farland stated further that:

> data was becoming available on the potential carcinogenicity associated with long-term exposure to lower frequency electromagnetic fields (EMF)... The evaluation of the possibility of human cancer risk is based on a judgment as to the overall weight of evidence that a carcinogenic response is causally related to specific levels or types of exposure... This evaluation confirms and extends the findings of other groups, including the Office of Technology Assessment (OTA), that a concern for potential carcinogenicity of EMF's

is emerging. Specifically, the report's conclusions are: several studies showing leukemia, lymphoma, and cancer of the nervous system in children exposed to magnetic fields from residential 60 Hertz electrical power distribution systems, and similar findings in adults in several occupational studies also involving electrical power frequency exposures, show a pattern of response which suggests, but does not prove a causal link. Evidence from a large number of biological test systems shows that these fields induce biological effects that are consistent with several possible mechanisms of carcinogenesis.

The EPA has prepared a report that examines and critically evaluates the relationships between exposure to EMF and cancer in humans. The workshop draft circulated for comment between June of 1990 and January 1993, indicates a strong link between EMF and cancer.

Other studies in this country between 1980 and 1985 have linked VDT's (Video Display Terminals used with computers-- CRTs) with 12 clusters of birth defects, stillbirth, and prematurity (spontaneous abortion or miscarriage). In a confirmed report spontaneous abortion in women exposed frequently to VDT's happens 10-15% of the time.

A study conducted, by the Kaiser Permanente Medical Care Plan, of women who were pregnant during the period 1981 and 1982 and exposed to malathion spraying in addition to spending at least 20 hours at a VDT, found an excess risk of miscarriage of 80%.

At Washington University in Seattle a team of scientists found that rats exposed to low level microwave radiation suffered four times as many malignant tumors than those that were not exposed.

Can Radiation be beneficial?

For decades, studies have shown that whenever one form of energy, such as EMF radiation, encounters another form of energy, such as human biological energy, changes inevitably occur. From all indications in studies conducted thus far, the kind of radiation that results from the use of 60 cycle alternating current, which is used exclusively in this country, can be extremely hazardous. But is all radiation harmful? Is it possible to produce beneficial radiation?

Early in this century, a handful of research scientists conducted intensive experiments exposing living tissue to a broad variety of vibrations ranging from high frequency, short wave radiation to low frequency, long wave radiation. They have found that when the radiation emits a frequency that is in harmony with specific living tissue, which radiates its own unique frequencies, an abatement of disease can take place.

Royal Reif's Discoveries

In the 1940's Dr. Royal R. Reif, a research scientist experimenting with the effects of electromagnetic radiation on living organisms, discovered that radiation of a specific frequency could destroy bacteria, yet leave other living tissues unharmed. He was extremely successful in destroying bacteria and viruses which were causing cancer and other illnesses.

Undaunted by his rejection by the AMA and more traditional practitioners, Reif and his associates continued to improve his frequency generator. Finally, in the 1960's, one of his units was presented to the California Public Health Department who tested it at the Palo Alto Detection Lab, the Kalbfeld Lab, the UCLA Medical Lab and the San Diego Testing Lab. The results of these tests proved the device safe to use.

Medical Doctors, researchers, clinics, and hospitals had all used the Reif device and displayed great enthusiasm over their results. Most who tested it were convinced of its ability to destroy cancer cells with a simple 3 minute application every third day. Complete cures had taken place in less than 3 months. In spite of Reif's initial success, the AMA banned use of the device. Eventually, the authorities invaded Reif's laboratory, destroyed his equipment and his records and arrested his associates. Reif is said to have died in prison.

Reif Rediscovered

For a time it was believed that the 50 years of valuable research by Reif was totally lost. Certain courageous physicians continued to defy the mandate of the AMA. Dr. Milbank Johnson, professor of physiology and clinical medicine at the University of Southern California, successfully treated cancer patients at his own clinic for the ten years preceding his death. After Johnson's death Dr. James Couche of San Diego took over his work and continued to use the Reif equipment for the next 22 years.

Testimonials

Much of the success attained through the use of the Reif generator is well documented by both doctors and patients. The list of doctors reads like a "Who's Who" of medical research. Dr. Couche was especially meticulous in recording his experiences with the Reif equipment. Excerpts from his records follow:

I would like to make this historical record of the amazing scientific wonders regarding the efficacy of the frequencies of the Royal R. Reif Frequency Instrument... In that period of time I saw many things and the one that impressed me the most was a man who staggered onto a table, just on the last end of cancer; he was a bag of bones. As he lay on the table, Dr. Reif said, 'Just feel that man's stomach.' So I put my hand on the cavity... this backbone and his belly were just about touching each other... However they gave him a treatment with the Reif frequencies and in the course of time over a period of six weeks to two months, to my astonishment, he completely recovered...

I saw some very remarkable things resulting from it in the course of over twenty years. I had a Mexican nine years of age, who had osteomyelitis of the leg. He was treated at the Mercy Hospital by his attending doctors. They scraped the bone every week. It was agonizing to the child because they never gave him anything; they just poked in there and cleaned him out and the terror of the boy was awful... His family brought him to my office. He was terrified that I would poke him as the other doctors had done. I reassured him and demonstrated the instrument on my own hand to show him that it would not hurt... In less than two weeks of treatment the wound was completely healed and he took off his splints and threw them away... He is a big powerful man now and has never had a comeback of his osteomyelitis. He was completely cured. There were many cases such as this.

Another user of the Reif Instrument, Dr. Charles Tulley of San Diego, has also recorded his experiences.

My first definite investigation was in that of my own case of prostatitis (inflammation of the prostate); I tried medicines. A qualified urologist gave me gantrisin, penicillin, aureomycin, chloromycin terramycin, with various results, but the drugs did not do the job. The Frequency Instrument cured my case quickly. I then used the Frequency Instrument on a friend of mine who was being rushed to the hospital for a prostate operation. He is perfectly well today without any operation or further medical aide.

I had a case of butterfly lupus sent to me by a doctor friend, and, though it had been treated extensively by specialists, the condition was large and in progression. After three months of treatment with the Frequency Instrument, the butterfly lupus disappeared.

Another cancer (carcinoma) case was submitted to me for treatment with the Frequency Instrument by an M.D. friend of mine. He had an impossible condition, but the Frequency Instrument dried it up in six weeks.

"I have found the Frequency Instrument very effective after surgery. I use it alone instead of antibiotics, and have not had a case of infection. I have cured extremely bad cases of trench mouth, and pyorrhea in a few treatments with the Frequency Instrument."

The following was recorded by George Chromiak, Jr., M.D.:

In the spring of 1960 I contacted a staph Aureus infection while an intern at St. Alexis Hospital in Cleveland, Ohio. This was a plague in this hospital as is still prevalent in most U.S. hospitals...difficult to control.

"The infection started with a throat culture which was suppressed with anti-biotics. Soon after, I with about six others became a victim of this anti-biotic-resistant infection which became systemic (effecting the entire body) and chronic.

"It was three years of suffering until I came across the Frequency Instrument which gave me immediate relief and control so that I was then on the road to a `CURE'."

Further Studies on EMR

In the meantime newer approaches to beneficial EMR have also been emerging. Since 1985 an independent research team in California has been conducting experiments to determine why radiation from ordinary household electricity is so harmful to human tissue. It has only been within the past few years that a major breakthrough has been made. They discovered that electric impulses generated by the brain that initiate the major functions of the body such as heartbeat, breathing, digestion, etc. are disrupted when bombarded by disordered, chaotic electromagnetic radiation found in American households.

An independent study of doctor's patients later revealed that patients who were exposed to EMR from household electricity did not respond well to the treatments by physicians. Whenever the source of the EMR could be located and removed, the patients regained their health. After many more years of study, devices that convert chaotic household current into beneficial electromagnetic radiation were developed.

Even more intense studies in EMR have been conducted, mainly outside of this country, on the beneficial effects of certain kinds of electromagnetic radiation. The applications of low frequency radiation to both humans and laboratory animals in Britain and Czechoslovakia have resulted in arresting a broad variety of illnesses. A Czech research team has developed an electromagnetic frequency generator that they applied to 84 cases of Multiple Sclerosis with a 95% success rate.

Private individuals experimenting with EMR as well as magnetism have produced a wide assortment of fascinating results. What is to follow are comments from a few of the people who had heard about the benefits of magnetic radiation and decided to test it:

E. P. went to Mexico to attend a seminar. Everyone in attendance got sick on the food except E. P. who exposed all of her food to magnetic radiation before eating it.

J. H. told of the mouse that had eaten the cheese he put out with arsenic in it. In just a few minutes the mouse looked dead. Out of curiosity he exposed the mouse to magnetic radiation. In a few hours the mouse was energetically trying to climb out of its cage.

Larry's son had a severe headache when he went to bed. Larry put a magnet under his pillow. When his son woke up a few hours later, his headache was gone.

A. I. closed a heavy metal door on his foot. The pain was unbearable. It began to swell almost immediately. After exposing it to magnetic radiation for one minute the pain was gone. After about an hour the swelling was gone.

A man in St. Paul Minnesota said a bird flew against his window. It appeared to be dead. This had happened many times before and none of the birds had recovered. Harry decided to expose the bird to magnetic radiation. He looked up 15 minutes later and the bird was gone.

One summer Sally picked some wild greens in the country. During the week, she periodically exposed the greens to magnetic radiation. At the end of the week the greens were as fresh as the day she picked them.

Dr. K.E.M. who was treating a patient with cancer, exposed him to magnetic fields. In addition to a cancer cure, the patient's hair was changed from silvery white to its original color.

L. T. had hundreds of ticks on his patio. He decided to line the patio with magnets. Within an hour there was not a tick to be found. He removed the magnets. The next day the ticks had returned.

S. E., who lived in an aluminum trailer, had a terrible problem with indigestion. He exposed the aluminum to magnetic radiation. He hasn't had a problem with indigestion since.

Harry's dog had a terrible case of fleas. He exposed his pet to magnetic radiation. Within minutes, he could find no fleas.

E. L. exposed his fresh produce, fruit and vegetables, to the north pole of a medium strength magnet. Normally most fruit spoiled before the end of the week. After exposure to magnetic radiation unrefrigerated fruit lasted several weeks. E. L. has also seen studies that show how all pollution can be eliminated when exposed to a magnetic field of the proper strength and frequency.

Wilma's grandchild stumbled onto an angry nest of yellow jackets and got stung many times. She exposed each sting to magnetic radiation. In less than a minute, the pain of the stings had stopped. The next day there was no sign of a sting at all.

L. D. glued low strength magnets to the frames of her glasses, and, after four months, her cataracts were gone.

Irma's grandmother had a very severe case of arthritis. It had been years since she was able to raise her arm above her shoulder. Irma exposed her grandmother's arm to magnetic radiation for about a half an hour. She could then raise her arm above her head with little pain.

A. T. exposed her young rubber plant to magnetic radiation and it grew over 14 inches in just three weeks. The plant that was not exposed grew only a few inches in the same amount of time.

P. R. straps magnets to his water pipes to purify and soften kitchen tap water.

D. C. never got more than 20 miles to the gallon on her full size 1978 Chevy. She placed magnets between the two front seats of her car over the gear box. On her next trip she carefully recorded her mileage and was amazed that her Chevy got over 30 miles per gallon.

Ethyl Starbard Neutralizing Pollution

In 1956, a lady by the name of Ethyl Starbard was a very sick woman. The diagnosis of her physician indicated that she had an intolerance of many pollutants found in the fresh fruit and vegetables she was eating.

She and her physician conducted a chemical analysis of supermarket fruit, namely apples, oranges and bananas. They tested for 20 pollutants. The apples they tested had all 20 pollutants, the oranges had 16, and the bananas had only 7. After exposure to North pole (counter-clockwise) energy, zero pollution was found. (See following table.)

Toxins	Apples	Oranges	Bananas	After Radiation
DDT	340	70	60	0
Dieldrin	45	30	40	0
Carbon Disulphide	10	20	18	0
Thorium	12	30	0	0
Ergot	12	18	0	0
Iodine	90	50	20	0
Carbon	55	35	0	0
Aluminum & Selenium	25	35	0	0
Holmium	25	0	0	0
Zirconium	15	2	0	0

Iridium	15	0	0	0
Caesium	20	15	0	0
Thallium	22	6	0	0
Molybdenum	20	0	0	0
Niobium	15	0	0	0
Botulinum	20	0	0	0
Cerium	12	18	0	0
Californium & Radium	50	12	0	0
Plutonium	20	50	20	0
Arsenic	50	40	20	0

Harmful vs Beneficial Radiation

Why is some magnetic radiation harmful and why are other's beneficial? There have been numerous experiments and theories over the years to attempt to answer this question. According to Ethel Starbard, who has been observing the effects of natural cosmic radiation since 1956, says it is due to the polarity of atomic radiation that determines whether it will be harmful or beneficial to humans.

Ethel believes that atoms in the cells of human tissue vibrate in a clockwise polarity. When the body is injured, or becomes ill, the atoms of the cells switch to counter-clockwise polarity. The exposure of injured tissue to atoms vibrating in a clockwise direction, as in natural radiation, will polarize the injured tissue to return to normal. Predatory insects, on the other hand, have atoms vibrating in a counter-clockwise direction and find it intolerable when exposed to a clockwise flow of atoms.

The Work of Hulda Clark

As early as the 1950s, Hulda Regehr Clark, Ph.D, N.D., has been studying biophysics, cell physiology and the effects of electromagnetic radiation on a broad spectrum of viruses, germs ,and fungi. In 1995 ProMotion Publishing of San Diego published her book *The Cure for All Diseases*. In this land mark publication she spelled out in precise detail what frequency of electromagnetic radiation would destroy which organism. She backs this up with dozens of stories about her experiences in applying specific frequencies to specific organisms and the results she achieved. (More on Dr. Clark in a later chapter)

Man-Made Destructive Power

The research team of a California based company that lead to several electromagnetic products have also suggested answers. Man made "EMR is inherently incompatible with living cells. The research focused on the fact that approximately 40% of the electrons in the physical world are essentially entropic in nature (i.e., disordered, random and chaotic)." The products of this company are designed to address this fundamental disorder and chaos by creating a degree of order in the electronic environment.

The publication Raum & Zeit expressed the idea in a similar way. "Most systems in the physical universe tend toward increasing positive entropy and more disorder over time. That is when things, apparatus, machines, and other inanimate objects tend to fall apart, chaos reigns. The most notable exception to this entropic rule of the physical universe is found in the behavior of living systems... Living systems display the property of negative entropy or a tendency toward decreasing disorder of the system," thus aging and illness occurs.

The Psychic Research Group, which also experimented with electromagnetism, writes that "Every particle, atom, molecule, organelle, cell, tissue, organ, and whole organism resonates at its own particular frequency. EEG measurements show that the field generated by the human brain has frequencies in the extremely low (ELF) region centering around 7 to 8 Hertz... It naturally resonates to, and is entrained by, the earth's resonant field, but can also be entrained by artificially generated fields of the appropriate frequencies... This "entrainment effect" can occur in every cell, organ and system of the body." In other words, if the resonant frequency of any magnetic field is in harmony with the resonant frequencies of the living organism, such as the earth's magnetic field, or Royal Reif's frequency generator, then this should be beneficial to living organisms. If, on the other hand, a resonant frequency is out of harmony with that of the living organism, as most manmade electromagnetic frequencies are, then this should be harmful to that organism. The decrease of the earth's magnetic field by 50% over the last 500 years could be one reason for the increase in the number of new health problems. The earth's field is also not constant. Its strength and frequency can range from less than one hertz (cycle per second) to over 30. This is a clue that the energy is entropic (disharmonious). This too could be causing health problems within specific geophysical or solar cycles. In fact links have been established between these cycles and the following:

1. Higher cardiovascular and cerebrovascular occurrences,
2. Higher number of outpatient heart attacks,
3. Higher than average blood pressure readings,
4. Higher concentration of blood platelet,
5. Higher blood plasma viscosity,
6. Higher levels of hormone secretions,
7. Effects on the central nervous system,
8. More severe migraine headaches,
9. More heart rhythm disturbances,
10. Higher mortality rates at hospitals.

Many of the experiences that have come to light recently may seem outrageous to some. The interest of an increasing number of credible organizations is being aroused. The Menninger Clinic of Topeka, Kansas which has been investigating subtle energies for the past 15 years is more recently focusing greater attention on EMR in our environment. Microsoft, Bill Gates' highly successful software development company, has been testing devices that alter the chaotic nature of VDT EMR. Sacramento, County of California, will also be testing similar devices.

Whether or not we are able to accept the idea of magnetism that can both heal and destroy the technology does appear to be gaining momentum. If appearances prove to be valid, EMR could radically change our attitudes toward a broad variety of established institutions: medicine, drugs, agriculture, and environmental protection. Who knows where it could lead us?

Clarus products offer some protection from many electronic transmissions. The Q-Link, for example, is designed to strengthen the personal aura. Other Clarus products build an electronic protection dome around the home similar to the electronic shield produced by the Starship Enterprise in the popular *Star Trek series*. Many of the technologies used in this series are becoming a reality today.

CHAPTER EIGHT

The Miracle-II Story

As many of my readers know I am continually researching new discoveries in the fields of health and technology. Many of these research projects have lead to successful products. One of these products is the phenomenonally successful Miracle-II. It is one of the few new products that I've had direct experience. I introduce it here because its success is primarily due to the Eloptic (electro-optical) energy in which these products are infused with. These are the scientific facts behind the development and phenomenal success of Miracle-II products. You will learn how a few, simple common sense changes incorporated in your daily hygiene regimen can have a profound and lasting impact on your health.

The Beginning

The Miracle II story begins in Louisiana with a man by the name of Clayton Tedeton. For over nine months he'd been suffering from the results of an automobile accident, unable to walk without losing his balance, hypersensitive to sound, and in almost constant pain. Then, after a night of desperate prayer, with the promise that he would "do whatever you want me to do" in return, Clayton woke up completely free of pain and full of energy. He'd experienced a miracle of healing.

Some years later he was mysteriously awakened at 1 AM. Drowsily, he opened his eyes. There scrawled in dazzling light across his bedroom wall were a series of words and symbols that Clayton did not understand. He decided it looked important enough to write down. After consulting scientists he learned that it was a formula that turned out to be the specifications for these amazing Miracle-II products. Shortly after these discoveries, he received the inner guidance to make these products available to the general public.

One of the first products Clayton developed was a soap used as an industrial cleanser. It turned out to be a powerful degreaser, and even a roach-killer as well. Then, people started reporting that the soap not only left their skin feeling really clean, but was also healing all kinds of skin conditions -- from burns to acne to psoriasis. After a while it was found that one part of the formula - the Neutralizer - could be taken internally and would aid in completely neutralizing many illnesses. (See www.Futeck.com for more information)

How I use the Miracle-II Neutralizer Internally

When I first started to use the Neutralizer, I was putting10 drops in water, juice, soup, any liquid, or whenever I consumed a liquid. Once I felt comfortable that I was not experiencing any healing crisis, I would increase the dosage gradually to 1/2 an ounce or more over a period of a year.

A healing crisis is the result of the body rejecting toxins that have accumulated over the years. It may take the form of an old problem illness from the past: joint pain, indigestion, cold or flu symptoms, etc. Unless they persist, this should not be a concern. It's a normal reaction. The dosage may be reduced or continued until the symptoms subside. I did experience a few minor discomforts, but they disappeared in a few days. After the healing crisis had passed, I increased the amount gradually. Right now I am taking as much as six ounces a day with no ill effects.

Clayton Tedeton, Miracle II's owner, believes it's not possible to have any adverse effects no matter how much you take. After 20 years of testing, this has proven to be true.

Since I started taking the Neutralizer I haven't had a cold, flu, or any other illnesses. It has been an amazing immune system booster. It seems to accomplish a similar function as the white blood cells by seeking out the body's invaders and neutralizing their effect.

Other Neutralizer Uses

I also use the Neutralizer as a mouth wash, undiluted -- full strength. I used to have a serious problem with pyorrhea and inflamed gums that would last for weeks. I seldom get it any more, and if I do, it never lasts long.

I also place Neutralizer into a spray bottle. I use this Neutralizer to spray in my ears when they get stopped up. It loosens the hard wax so it may be removed easily. Since I've been spraying it on my hair, it has turned darker and I have much less hair loss. I am hopeful that I may grow some new hair eventually. It also eliminates static cling.

According to the owner, Miracle II Neutralizer cleans out the veins of plaque and debris, oxygenates and alkalizes the blood.

I put an ounce of Neutralizer in a gallon of water along with an ounce of Miracle II soap. This I spray on my plants to destroy fungus and repel insects. Growth seems to be better also.

Miracle-II Neutralizer Gel

I've had excellent success using the Neutralizer Gel. When I returned from the Health Expo in Washington DC last year, my muscles were so stiff and cramped I could hardly stand up. I rubbed a generous portion of the Gel on them and within a minute the cramps were gone, never to return that day.

A few mornings ago I got out of bed with such back pain that I couldn't stand up straight. I rubbed Gel on the muscles that were hurting and within a minute I was able to straighten up. I gave a second application about an hour later, and the pain disappeared entirely. It was the muscles in my sides and back that caused the pain. If the pain is caused by a joint problem it will take much longer – probably months.

The Gel also seems to be effective for virtually any skin problem. I've used it for fungus, insect bites, skin rash, itching skin, scaling skin, and many others. Clayton (the owner) says it's also good for acne, age spots, athletes foot, bed sores, burns & cuts, bruises, Candida, Cellulite, complexion, dandruff, Diaper rash, dry skin, fever blisters, Hemorrhoids, Herpes, Hives, Gout, Jock itch, poison Ivy/Oak, and psoriasis.

I also use the Gel as a toothpaste, one dab of the Gel and one drop of the Miracle II soap. My teeth have never felt cleaner or looked whiter. My dentist had been commenting that he would have to do something about my receding gums. During my last visit he seemed surprised how well that problem was solving itself.

I've also heard that the Gel dissolves plaque. During my last cleaning, the dental assistant found very little plaque when she cleaned my teeth, so the "dissolve plaque" rumor must be true. I am very happy with the effectiveness of the Gel and the Neutralizer as a mouthwash.

Recently, I started to use the Gel as a body lotion before I apply the Miracle-II skin moisturizer. My skin seems smother and the finer wrinkles seem to be less.

The owner of the Miracle-II formula, has told me many stories about the users of the Gel. He just recently began to market the products in Saudi Arabia where Ringworm is epidemic. Even the Camels have it. They are spreading the Gel on the infection daily and the problem disappears in less than 2 weeks. It's been the only 100% effective product against ringworm.

He also said the daughter of one of the Sheiks had an extremely painful third degree burn. They applied the Gel and in just a few days a scab had formed. A few days later the scab fell off and underneath was new, completely healed skin.

I recently learned that the Neutralizer has 10 times more neutralizing energy than the soaps and the moisturizing lotion, and that the Gel has 4 times more neutralizing energy than the Neutralizer. This would certainly account for the incredible effectiveness of the Gel.

Miracle-II Moisturizing Soap

I use this soap for all my personal cleansing: shower, shampoo, etc. Regular soap used to make my skin very dry and make it scaly. Miracle II makes my skin silky smooth. For anyone who has oily skin I would suggest the regular non-moisturizing soap. Another interesting side effect is that my shower never gets that soapy scum or fungus on the walls. Miracle II keeps my shower and tub clean.

Miracle-II Non-Moisturizing Soap

I use this soap for all of my household cleaning chores: dishes, laundry (if you don't have a Miracle II laundry ball that replaces detergents), oven, counter top, rug shampoo, auto wash, etc.

The Miracle-II Skin Moisturizer

The high energy of this lotion penetrates the skin and the high quality oils help iron out the fine wrinkles.

Miracle-II Deodorant

This deodorant is one of the very few non-toxic deodorants on the market. Most deodorants have toxic aluminum that some believe are a major factor in the cause of breast cancer.

CHAPTER NINE

The Body Snatchers - Part I
Introduction

Much of my spare time over the last 20 years has focused on the question: "How can I promote my own physical, mental and spiritual well being?" For many of those 20 years, however, the focus has been on the health of the physical body--primarily dealing with learning about its functions and its needs which I have been sharing with the readers of the Future Technologies Newsletter since January of 1998.

It was in 1995 that I began to realize the devastating impact the environment has been having on my health. I took university courses on ecology, studied pollution's impact on the environment and how this devastating trend might be reversed. With books like *Silent Spring* by Rachel Carson as a source, we now know that a major portion of this pollution comes from our generation and its use of toxic sources of energy. I studied the dozens of ways that we could generate clean, environmentally friendly energy.

Then in 1997 Dennis Lee, inventor, researcher, and former industrialist, came to town claiming he had the solutions to all of our pollution problems. In his research lab, he said he was developing six different technologies that generate free energy for our homes and cars, including the technology of genius, Nikola Tesla. Unfortunately, his dream never materialized due to more powerful forces in government and industry that prevented it.

While much of my early research focused on the environment, my ultimate goal has always been physical and mental health. The tale that I have to weave in this chapter is both educational and scary. It really began back in June of 2000. I was conducting research for the upcoming newsletter in July. I shared some of my research on the endocrine systems--probably the most important system in our bodies--a knowledge of which general practicing physicians know relatively little about. That July 2000 newsletter contained only an overview of the extensive research that I conducted.

The Endocrine System

As you may recall, the endocrine system consists of a chain of seven major ductless glands along with all the complex nerve connections that constantly interact with each other. These consist of the Pituitary and Pineal (located in the head), the thyroid (located in the neck), the Thymus (located over the heart), the two Adrenals (located to the left and right sides of the back), and the gonads (located below the abdomen). This system of glands and nerves literally control every function in the body. This is a scientifically deduced fact. The malfunction of any one of these glands can cause serious imbalance in any of the body's systems.

Thyroid

While I was researching the Thyroid gland I stumbled onto the Web site of Mary Shamon (http://thyroid.about.com/) whose focus is exclusively thyroid problems. In her Web site she has a wealth of information on the thyroid, but the page that hit me between the eyes was a page listing the possible symptoms of hypothyroidism. The writer advised that if we can say "yes" to three or four of these symptoms, we should be tested for a hypothyroidism. Here is the list:

I am gaining weight inappropriately
I'm unable to lose weight with diet/exercise

I am constipated, sometimes severely

I have low body temperature (I feel cold when others feel hot, need extra sweaters, socks)

I feel fatigued, exhausted at times

I Feel run down, sluggish, lethargic

My hair is coarse and dry, breaking, brittle, or falling out

My skin is coarse, dry, scaly, or thick

I have a hoarse or gravely voice

I have puffiness and swelling around the eyes and face

I have pains, aches in joints, hands and feet

I have developed carpal-tunnel syndrome, or it's getting worse

I am having irregular menstrual cycles (longer, or heavier, or more frequent)

I am having trouble conceiving a baby

I feel depressed

I feel restless

My moods change easily

I have feelings of worthlessness

I have difficulty concentrating

I have more feelings of sadness

I seem to be losing interest in normal daily activities

I'm more forgetful lately

The following symptoms have been reported most frequently in people with hypothyroidism (the thyroid isn't producing enough of its hormone):

My hair is falling out

I can't seem to remember things

I have no sex drive

I am getting more frequent infections, that last longer

I'm snoring more lately

I have/may have sleep apnea (stop breathing
   repeatedly during sleep)
I feel shortness of breath and tightness in the chest
I feel the need to yawn to get oxygen
My eyes feel gritty and dry
My eyes feel sensitive to light
My eyes get jumpy/tics in eyes, which makes me
dizzy/vertigo and have headaches
I have strange feelings in neck or throat
I have tinnitus (ringing in ears)
I get recurrent sinus infections
I have vertigo
I feel some lightheadedness
I have severe menstrual cramps

I was shocked to learn that I had, periodically experienced at least half of the symptoms listed for hypothyroidism. My first thought was to search for a natural remedy. I found several, tried them for almost a year, and then gave up. None made a difference, so I began to wonder whether my symptoms were really related to the thyroid.

I went to a traditional medical doctor for testing. It was an extensive battery of blood tests over a period of several months that cost nearly $2000. The tests were all negative (Thyroid is fully functional), yet I still had an intuitive sense that thyroid was the problem. I continued my research, and months later I received the quarterly Edgar Cayce Book Catalogue. In the catalogue was a book dealing exclusively with thyroid research called *Thyroid Power* by Drs. Richard and Karilee Shames.

I learned three vital bits of information from this book: 1. Thyroid tests of the medical profession are often inaccurate due to the excessively wide range of acceptable readings, and 2. thyroid problems are, more frequently than not, caused by heavy metals--mercury in particular--accumulating in the glands and other body parts, and 3. Considering the complex interaction taking place among all of the Endocrine System components, the root cause may not lay with the Thyroid at all. The root cause could be with another endocrine gland or in the nervous system.

These were major discoveries in my quest for a solution. I decided to ask my dentist at the next checkup about mercury in my dental fillings. He confirmed that a major cause of thyroid impairment, as well as many other health problems, is mercury, as well as other heavy metals in the body.

My dentist recommended a naturopathic physician where I could get tests for heavy metals. I followed his advice, and after another battery of blood tests and another thousand or more dollars, nothing was proven, except when the heavy metals urine test came back from the lab, I discovered that I had 24 heavy metals in me, 12 of which were in the danger area: lead, mercury, barium, chromium, copper, gallium, lithium, manganese, nickel, rubidium, titanium, and tungsten. Two of those twelve were off the chart completely - nickel and lithium. Naturally, I began to wonder how these metals are getting into my body.

I decided to check the EPA (Environmental Protection Agency) Web site to see what research they have done. I found a link there (www.scorecard.org/chemical-profiles/ probably an EPA contractor) that included some incredibly extensive research into environmental pollutants. Scorecard provides detailed information on more than 6,800 chemicals (www.scorecard.org/chemical-profiles/def/universe.html), including all the chemicals used in large amounts in the United States or Canada and all the chemicals regulated under major environmental laws. You simply search for information by typing in the chemical's name.

Scorecard catalogued over 650 pollutants in our environment and listed their health effects. I randomly reviewed about 50 of them. Of the 50, 49 were known carcinogens, plus numerous others were suspected of causing other illnesses. Many of the metals were suspected of disabling the endocrine and immune systems entirely (governed by the thymus gland). For each pollutant Scorecard also ranked how dangerous it is to the health. Aluminum, arsenic, lead, mercury, and nickel were among the most hazardous metals.

Scorecard also covers how much of these metals are being produced, which industry produces them, and in which products these metals may be found. It also lists geographical areas, facilities or industrial sectors reporting the largest releases, federal regulatory coverage and valuable links to other sites.

As it appears from this incredibly detailed research I, along with millions of others in our country, are being constantly bombarded by an environment that is slowly killing us. I will wager a guess that most of our population has about the same or similar pollutants in their bodies as I do. And Maryland, according to scorecard.org, is ranked as having only average pollution among the 50 states. Many other states are subject to much higher pollution than Maryland.

I was particularly interested in environmental toxicants in Maryland that were particularly damaging to the endocrine system. Here are the toxicants found in air and water starting with the heaviest concentrations: lead, arsenic, styrene, and others (11 in all). Toxicants that affect the endocrine's immune function were also listed: xylene, toluine, nickel, zinc, lead, cobalt and others (17 in all). The vital neurological system is affected by 63 different toxicants in Maryland including manganese, barium, lead, nickel, arsenic, selenium, cyanide, tolulene, xylene, aluminum, and others. Virginia and Pennsylvania were very similar to Maryland. The District of Columbia, however, had fewer heavy metals than Maryland, Virginia or Pennsylvania, probably due to the lack of heavy industrial polluters.

Since I cannot protect myself while I am out in the open air, I have been doing all I can to protect myself in my own controlled environment. I have been drinking either filtered or distilled water for about 5 years. I have been eating organic foods whenever I can get them for about 3 years, and I have been filtering and oxygenating my air for over a year.

How are all of these heavy metals getting into my body after I've been so conscientious about avoiding them, or have they already been there for 20 years or more? How are they affecting my hormone balance and my endocrine and neurological systems that are inseparably linked to all of my body systems? What are the health effects that result from the impairment of these vital body systems? How may these impairments be corrected? These will be subjects for upcoming chapters.

CHAPTER TEN

Body Snatchers - Part II

Why do I consider this chapter the most important that I have ever written? These reasons!

Family physicians

When I recall my experiences over the past 30 years or more, I begin to realize evermore strongly just how much my family physicians did not know. This very frequently applies to traditional specialists, naturopaths, and alternative practitioners as well.

When I look back on the history of my interaction with traditional medical practitioners and their misdiagnoses of migraines, ADD (Attention Deficit Disorder), Manic Depression, and countless other illnesses, and when I recall the neglect, the lack of concern, the wrong prescriptions, the taking of dozens of pills and bad tasting liquids—the list is endless—I begin to wonder what other courses are available to me.

The first thought that came to me was to always get a second, third or more opinion. I also learned not to restrict myself to traditional medicine. I've visited naturopaths, homeopaths, nutritionists, acupuncturists, chiropractors, and body workers.

What kind of evidence do I have that this is good policy for every part of me? Have you ever gone to a doctor, spent thousands of dollars on visits and blood tests only to hear that there is nothing wrong with you, or "it's all in your mind?" I have, and more than once. Have you ever taken pills and horrible tasting liquids for months, or even years, and still felt bad? I have, and more than once. In a 1999 report, the Institute of Medicine estimated that as many as 98,000 Americans die every year because of medical errors. The figures are much higher today.

Never be afraid of offending your family physician by getting a second or third opinion. This is your life and wellbeing we're talking about.

A study by the National Council on Patient Information and Education showed that at least 125,000 people each year die from prescription drugs their doctors never should have given them because they had pre-existing conditions that are clearly contraindicated in the drugs' packaging. Many people naturally trust their doctors and pharmacists to prevent these kinds of problems. Other studies have shown that, more than ever, each of us has to be our own watchdog.

Another problem with traditional medical practice is their lack of continuing study. Most don't keep up with the latest research -- especially in the areas of alternative practices. New discoveries occur all of the time. For most doctors, the only new technology they learn about is from the drug companies. Therefore, it's always "more of the same;" treating only symptoms with toxic drugs that cause one or more secondary symptoms. More than one person I've known are taking 12 or more drugs and still feeling bad.

Drugs and the FDA

The FDA was brought into existence to protect us against unsavory companies that might produce health care products harmful to the public. An article in the Journal of American Medical Association (AMA) stated that approximately 106,000 deaths occur each year in U.S. hospitals because of adverse reactions to prescription drugs which were "used as directed." These are only the deaths that take place under close hospital staff supervision and do not include those who died at home that many feel could be considerably higher.

For years now drug companies have been pressuring congress to pass laws that make vitamin/mineral supplements and herbal remedies prescription medicines. The drug companies lobby for them intensely. They're loosing hundreds of billions of dollars a year to alternative health care. We are hitting their bottom line and they want relief. Some time ago the European Parliament passed the "European Union Directive on Dietary Supplements" which classifies supplements as medical drugs rather that food supplements. Many supplements will no longer be available over-the-counter in Europe. Many supplements in this country come from overseas. I frequently order alternative products from Europe that are not available here. This will affect us directly. Even more scary, U.S. congress has at least a dozen similar bills that have been circulating through the approval process for years.

Pollution

When doctors ask for lab tests they practically never consider the effects of pollution on the health of their patients. This is a serious failing. The studies that have been arranged by the EPA (Environmental Protection Agency) prove that over 640 chemicals have been found in our environment, most of which have been shown, or suspected, to be damaging to our health. I realize how unrealistic it would be to test for 640 pollutants, but there is sufficient public-access information to narrow a specific set of symptoms to manageable number of elements for testing. A good heavy metals test should be mandatory, yet few physicians request them. It's not an expensive test (mine cost $100). Blood tests routinely ordered by doctors can run into the thousands of dollars before they're finished, and in my recent experience, they didn't discover anything related to my symptoms.

Last April when I first suspected that I may have hypothyroidism, at the encouragement of a friend, I visited a medical doctor for the first time in over 30 years. Most of the lab tests he requested were to determine whether certain elements that are normally found in the body are within tolerance. He never tested for toxic environmental pollutants that shouldn't be there and have a potential to do serious harm.

The Endocrine System

As I've mentioned numerous times before in my newsletters, I consider the endocrine system to be the most important system in the body. Why? Because this system, in cooperation with our complex network of nerves, synapses, ganglion and the brain, affects every function in the body. Here is another area where family physicians are seriously lacking in sufficient knowledge to serve their patients effectively. It is also a system that is seldom, if ever, given sufficient attention by most physicians when diagnosing a group of symptoms. The physician I consulted last April initially requested a battery of lab tests, none of which tested the thyroid. It was only after he didn't find any serious abnormalities initially that he consented to do one, and only after I suggested it. I don't believe he would have ever requested it on his own. To his credit, he finally admitted that he didn't have sufficient knowledge to make an accurate diagnosis and suggested a specialist whom he said would probably charge about $600 per visit. I decided to do my own research instead.

Within the last few years I've begun to treat my symptoms as exciting adventures and opportunities for learning new things. I now have enough confidence to do this, but only after I was able to dissolve my fears of illness and death. I can do this comfortably with a chronic illness, but not a serious one.

I have discussed the potentially devastating health effects of heavy metals such as mercury, lead, aluminum, nickel, chromium, barium, and others. I still had unanswered questions:

How are these toxic metals getting into our bodies?
What kinds of symptoms do they produce?
What harm are they doing to our bodies?
What role does the endocrine system play?
How are heavy metals affecting those functions?

How do those malfunctions affect other vital functions of our body (e.g., our cardiovascular system, pulmonary system, digestive system, nervous system and even our mental/emotions abilities? What can we do about it?

The Cure for all Diseases

Dr. Hulda Regehr Clark, author, health researcher, and lecturer, after receiving her Bachelors Degree in Canada, came to the U.S. to study physiology. She earned her doctorate in that subject at the University of Minnesota in 1958 with majors in cell physiology and biophysics. Biophysics is "the study of biological phenomenon using the principles and techniques of physics" (Webster). Dr. Clark used these skills to catalogue many of the frequencies of pathogens that cause most of the world's diseases. In 1979 she left government funded research to open a private consulting practice. A few years later she published her books *The Cure for all Cancers and The Cure for HIV and Aids. The Cure for all Diseases,* her latest ground-breaking book, she wrote the following:

No matter how long and confusing is the list of symptoms a person has, from chronic fatigue to infertility to mental problems, I am sure to find only two things wrong: they have in them pollutants and/or parasites. I never find lack of exercise, vitamin deficiencies, hormone levels or anything else to be a primary causative factor. . . It's a valiant quest: The quest for health. With optimism in one hand and determination in the other, you too can work miracles for yourself that my clients accomplished in the case histories (numerous documented accounts may be found in Dr. Clark's books). More good news is that it is not expensive. The cost will range from a few hundred dollars to only a few thousand in order to eliminate both problems and cure your chronic diseases.

CHAPTER ELEVEN

The Body Snatchers – Part III

Our last chapter ended with a quote from Dr. Hulda Clark's groundbreaking work *The Cure for all Diseases*. It was such an incredible revelation for me that I'd like to reinforce it here.

No matter how long and confusing is the list of symptoms a person has, from chronic fatigue to infertility to mental problems, I am sure to find only two things wrong: they have in them pollutants and/or parasites. I never find lack of exercise, vitamin deficiencies, hormone levels or anything else to be a primary causative factor. . . It's a valiant quest: The quest for health. With optimism in one hand and determination in the other, you too can work miracles for yourself that my clients accomplished in the case histories (numerous documented accounts may be found in Dr. Clark's books). More good news is that it is not expensive. The cost will range from a few hundred dollars to only a few thousand in order to eliminate both problems and cure your chronic diseases.

Heavy Metals Pollution

When Dr. Clark talks about pollution she is referring primarily to heavy metals pollution. When we look at the Periodic Table of Elements, we notice that all but about six (hydrogen, nitrogen, Oxygen, helium...) are considered heavy metals.

The first thing I wondered was: how are toxic metals getting into my body and what symptoms are they producing? My first answer to this question came when I first read the book *The Cure for all Diseases* by Dr. Clark.

Early in her studies, Dr. Clark learned that all of the parasites and pollutants that cause illness have a vibration with a unique frequency. She knew that if she could isolate each pathogen that she found in patients with cancer, H.I.V. Aids, heart disease, diabetes, stroke, and other serious illnesses, this could be a giant step in the direction of finding a cure. Through her years of research she was able to catalogue the frequencies of thousands of parasites and pollutants. Among the pollutants she found over 30 heavy metals. I'll mention only those that she found most consistently in her patients, and were the most damaging to our health. These include aluminum, arsenic, barium, chromium, copper, lead, mercury, and nickel.

As many of you are aware, most of these elements are required by the body, but as Dr. Clark has stated in her book, *The Cure for All Diseases*, they must be in organic form. When found on the supermarket or drugstore shelf, they are practically never labeled organic, meaning relatively free of inorganic metals. This is the reason Dr. Clark states that many supplements do more harm than good: "Biochemists know that a mineral in raw element form always inhibits the enzyme using that mineral. Copper (for example) from the meat and vegetables you eat are essential. Inorganic copper, like you would get from a copper-bottomed kettle or copper plumbing, is carcinogenic. Unfortunately, the inorganic form of metals is what pervades our environment."

Aluminum is suspected of being a cardiovascular and blood toxicant, neurotoxicant, and respiratory toxicant (according to the EPA).

Aluminum gets into the body when we wrap our food in aluminum foil, cook our food in aluminum pots and pans, drink our soft drinks from aluminum cans, shake our salt from plastic salt shakers or bake our cakes with baking powder. Several years ago I decided to list ingredients that I found in personal care products I found on drugstore shelves. Every deodorant on the shelf contained inorganic aluminum. Several research studies showed that aluminum deodorants may be the cause of breast cancer and Alzheimer's disease. Research has shown that the body absorbs metal molecules merely by touching them.

Arsenic is recognized as a carcinogen, and developmental toxicant, and is suspected of being a cardiovascular and blood toxicant, gastrointestinal and liver toxicant, Kidney toxicant, neurotoxicant, respiratory toxicant, plus skin and sense organ toxicant (according to the EPA).Arsenic may get into the body through our food, air (used in pesticides), lawns treated with herbicides and pesticides, our furniture, and carpets that are treated with stain resistant chemicals.

Barium is suspected of being developmental toxicant, neurotoxicant, and respiratory toxicant (according to the EPA).

Barium may be found primarily in women's lipstick, but has also been found in some cosmetics, dental fillings, and gas engine exhaust fumes.

Dr. Clark has named chromium (along with nickel) as the most carcinogenic metal in the Periodic Table. It is also suspected of being a cardiovascular and blood toxicant, developmental toxicant, gastrointestinal and liver toxicant, reproductive toxicant, and respiratory toxicant (according to the EPA).

Chromium is often found in dental fillings, eyebrow pencil, and water softening salts. Stainless steel cookware contains 18% chromium and 8% nickel. So "throw those metal pots away," says Dr. Clark. "All metal seeps" into our foods.

Copper has been known to cause, cancer, leukemia, schizophrenia, high blood pressure, and infertility. Dr Clark found copper in all cancerous tumors that she tested. "This makes plumbing the second greatest hazard," --next to mercury -- says Dr. Clark. Copper is also a cardiovascular and blood toxicant, developmental toxicant, gastrointestinal and liver toxicant, reproductive toxicant, and respiratory toxicant (according to the EPA). Copper can be found in some tooth fillings, copper pots and pans, and copper plumbing of older houses.

Lead is a known carcinogen, developmental toxicant, and reproductive toxicant. It is suspected of being a cardiovascular and blood toxicant, endocrine toxicant, gastrointestinal and liver toxicant, Immunotoxicant, kidney toxicant, neurotoxicant, respiratory toxicant, skin, and sense organ toxicant. Lead toxicity also often causes leg cramps or spasms, and lowers the body's immune defenses (according to the EPA).Lead may be found in soldered or galvanized plumbing, automobile exhaust, and some paints.

Mercury is a recognized developmental toxicant and suspected of being a cardiovascular and blood toxicant, developmental toxicant, endocrine toxicant, gastrointestinal and liver toxicant, kidney toxicant, neurotoxicant, reproductive toxicant, and respiratory toxicant. It is suspected of penetrating, and impairing the function of virtually every cell in the body including the brain. Neuropsychiatric symptoms include; insomnia, nervousness, hallucinations, memory loss, headache, dizziness, anxiety, irritability, drowsiness, emotional instability, depression, and poor cognitive function (according to the EPA).

The American Dental Association's (ADA) long-standing policy has been that mercury poses no health risk and has, in the past ridiculed, and even destroyed the careers, of dentists who objected to their advice. And "The attitude of the majority of dentists," says Dr. Clark, "is: whatever (ADA) says is OK, they will do. The more reasonable philosophy is that there is no tooth worth saving if it damages your immune system."

This is the reason that Dr. Clark often suggests to her patients that removal of mercury fillings be the first course of action in any healing modality. In addition to amalgam fillings, mercury may also infect the body from ingested fish and seafood, pesticides, laxatives, batteries, paper and pulp products, drinking water, and paint products.

Nickel is a known carcinogen. It is suspected of being a cardiovascular and blood toxicant, developmental toxicant, immunotoxicant, kidney toxicant, neurotoxicant, reproductive toxicant, respiratory toxicant, skin, and sense organ toxicant (according to the EPA).

Nickel can get into the body through amalgam fillings and cosmetics (check your ingredients). Nickel is found in the soil and usually clings to vegetables in microscopic quantities. Stainless steel is 8% nickel and it is found in your knives, forks, and spoons. Many foods interact with the metal. You can often taste it. Bacteria in your body need nickel to survive. When you eat with metal flatware, you are helping bacteria destroy your own body. Chicken feed also has nickel, so eating chicken or chicken eggs puts nickel into the body. Oils on your skin dissolve nickel in metal jewelry, watches, and metal eyeglasses, transporting it into the body. Once you get all the nickel out of your body, you might begin to notice hair beginning to fill in the bald spots. You can also stop prostate problems dead in their tracks by eliminating nickel pollution of your body. To get rid of nickel already in the body, Dr. Clark recommends 500mg. of histidine once a day for three weeks. Histidine is an effective nickel chelator.

It's All In Your Head
Dr. Hal A. Huggins, author of *It's all in Your Head* received his DDS from the University of Nebraska. Since 1962 he has practiced general dentistry with an emphasis on nutrition. In 1973 he became involved in the study of mercury toxicity and its impact on human health. Through the course of his investigation of the mechanisms of toxicity as they relate to auto-immune disease, Dr. Huggins earned a Master of Science from the University of Colorado at Colorado Springs. In 1983, Dr. Huggins began a full time practice devoted to diagnosing

and planning treatment for patients suffering from mercury toxicity.

During his research to discover why mercury is so devastating to the health, Dr Huggins discovered that the mercury itself does not cause illness, but rather it's the electromagnetic energy emanating from the mercury. The following is an excerpt from his groundbreaking text.

> Mercury [energy] kills cells by interfering with their ability to exchange oxygen, nutrients, and waste through the cell membrane. Inside the cell, mercury destroys our genetic code, DNA, leaving us without the ability to reproduce that cell ever again. Immunologically, mercury embeds itself in a cell membrane, giving the cell the appearance of being a 'nonself,' which is the trigger for the immune system to destroy that specific cell. With mercury in your cell membranes, the immune system will start destroying your own tissues, thus the term autoimmune disease... Mercury can interfere with nerve impulse transmissions, causing organs to get wrong messages. This may be related to frequent memory problems... Mercury can become attached to hormones and deactivate them, even though blood tests say that plenty of hormone is present. Many hormonal deficiencies, including thyroid, pancreas, and sex hormones, are the result of this process... When mercury interferes with energy production and oxygen transport, all cells are affected.

"Eureka!" I said to myself when I first read these paragraphs. Here is the cause of every symptom I've ever had over the past 40 years -- The hypoglycemia, the hypothyroidism, the allergies, the chronic fatigue, the poor memory, the shortness of breath, the dry skin, the hair loss, the cold extremities, and dozens of symptoms too numerous to mention.

CHAPTER TWELVE

The Body Snatchers - Part IV

This <u>Body Snatchers</u> series was based, to a large degree, on the groundbreaking research of Dr. Hulda Clark as it was documented in her book *The Cure for all Diseases*. Once again I would like to repeat that paragraph that so impressed my brain.

"No matter how long and confusing is the list of symptoms a person has, from chronic fatigue to infertility to mental problems, I am sure to find only two things wrong: they have in them pollutants and/or parasites. I never find lack of exercise, vitamin deficiencies, hormone levels or anything else to be a primary causative factor.

I would also like to reinforce a paragraph from the book of Dr. Hal A. Huggins, author of It's all In Your Head. During his research to discover why mercury is so devastating to our health, Dr Huggins wrote the following:

Mercury [energy] kills cells by interfering with their ability to exchange oxygen, nutrients, and waste through the cell membrane" wrote Dr. Huggins. "Inside the cell, mercury destroys our genetic code, DNA, leaving us without the ability to reproduce that cell ever again. Immunologically, mercury embeds itself in a cell membrane, giving the cell the appearance of being a 'non-self,' which is the trigger for the immune system to destroy that specific cell. With mercury in your cell membranes, the immune system will start destroying your own tissues, thus the term autoimmune disease... Mercury can interfere with nerve impulse transmissions, causing organs to get wrong messages. This may be related to frequent memory problems. Mercury can become attached to hormones and deactivate them, even though blood tests say that plenty of hormone is present. Many hormonal deficiencies, including thyroid, pancreas, and sex hormones, are the result of this process... When mercury interferes with energy production and oxygen transport, all cells are affected.

Heavy Metal Remedies

When I first tested positive for 24 different heavy metals, I was being treated by a medical doctor who had a strong background in alternate methods of treatment. Unfortunately, she had no experience with riding the body of heavy metals. This led me to suspect that most physicians would be of little help, since it's not in their traditional procedure or training to test or treat for the symptoms of pollution or parasites in the body or to rid the body of them.

Many remedies have been suggested by those who have done the groundbreaking research for chelation or removal of heavy metals.

If a patient of Dr. Clark had metal fillings in their teeth, her first suggested remedy would be to replace the filing with nontoxic ceramic or glass fillings. Since few people can afford this process, I suggest the faithful ingestion of Miracle-II Neutralizer. If you can't remove the hazard, Miracle-II will at least reduce or neutralize mercury's harmful affect.

Secondly, Dr. Clark might suggest a patient remove heavy metals, as much as possible from their life: aluminum, copper or stainless steal pots, pans, or flatware (refer to previous chapters for the sources of heavy metal pollution.).

For removing heavy metals that are already in the body, Dr. Clark suggested EDTA (*ethylene diamine tetra ocetate*) chelation therapy. This can be an expensive and time-consuming remedy If taken intravenously, but effective, according to Dr. Clark. I recently had a heavy metals test then ten injections (the first stage of the series that could reach 40). I had to pay for the test ($300) and the actual chelation was partially covered by Medicare. They will pay for the treatment if your level of lead in above the danger point, which for most of us, it is.

Oral EDTA chelation is also available which is much less expensive and more convenient. Its effectiveness has been debated.

Researchers have found that chelators such as DMPS or DMSA also are effective in certain individuals. Some researchers believe DMSA has less adverse side effects than DMPS.

Natures Sunshine, after years of research, have introduced an herbal Heavy Metal Detox product. This is one of the more reputable companies in the field. I've been using their products for years, and I find them extremely effective.

Dr. Mercola (http://www.mercola.com/), a respected MD who has done extensive research in many forms of alternative cures has suggested Chlorella as a powerful metal detoxifying agent. Here is what Dr. Mercola says about Chlorella:

> As foods go, chlorella is among the elite few that reside in the "Near Perfect" category. For a simple single cell algae plant coming from fresh water, chlorella's range of benefits is astounding. Chlorella will: help your body remove the heavy metals and other pesticides in your body, improve your digestive system, including decreasing constipation, focus more clearly and for greater duration balance your body's pH, and help eliminate bad breath.
> (http://www.mercola.com/chlorella/index.htm)

We must be aware that a remedy that works for one person, may not work for another. We are breaking new ground here, and I usually keep trying the different remedies until I find one that works for me.

A few years ago I had all my metal fillings removed. It was very expensive, but, in my opinion, worth the cost. I realize that many cannot afford the cost. It was difficult for me. My Dentist

(Dr William DeLong of Columbia, MD) said the element Mercury is not what causes the damage to our health, but rather the electromagnetic energy that it radiates. Here is another, and, possibly, the most important benefit of the Miracle-II Neutralizer. If the Neutralizer's powerful energy can neutralize anthrax and many other toxic, wartime chemicals, it can surely neutralize electromagnetic energy of most heavy metals that get into the body.

Getting Rid of Parasites

Dr. Clark has detailed two primary methods for destroying and expelling parasites from the body.

She has done more research on detecting and destroying parasites than anyone else I know. She has catalogued the energy frequencies for hundreds of different parasites. She also discovered that she could destroy the parasite if she subjected it to a specific frequency. Over the years she has been improving her electronic unit she calls "The Zapper" which will destroy many of the more common parasites. She has detailed plans for building her Zapper in her book *The Cure for all Diseases*. She also sells an advanced version of her Zapper that may be found on her Web site (www.drclark,com).

The second method that Dr. Clark suggests for destroying parasites is an herbal one. Most importantly she recommends black walnut hulls in combination with the herbs cloves and wormwood. She now has an extra-strength black walnut hull tincture that is effective against most parasites.

CHAPTER THIRTEEN

Digging Up Roots - Part 1

When it comes to the cause for illness, the pressures in our lives, or any health problem, the roots run deep. This is the reason that total cures are seldom achieved, and we expire before our time. It's true that we have achieved some success through diets, herbs, homeopathy, osteopathy, and some may even say allopathy (practice of today's MDs). Seldom have these cures resolved the "root" cause. "Why?" is the question I plan to address in this series *Digging Up Roots.*

Where Did We Go Wrong?
"I never let my schooling interfere with my education," quipped the wise American humorist and author, Mark Twain. Considering the numerous controversies over today's educational methods, the words of the beloved Mark Twain seem to arouse the same knowing chuckles that they did in the 20th century consciousness. Why do we educate? What should we teach, and how should we teach it? These questions seem to be ever-present thorns in the sides of many progressive educators of our time. Many feel that our institutions have failed to prepare us for the more difficult encounters with life.

Most will admit that the best way to acquire knowledge is through direct experience. Yet, now more than ever, current teaching methods seem to stress an unwritten code that "words impart knowledge." To know something is to have a clear perception of it. How clear is our perception of a truth that is drawn from the words on a page or from the mouth of a teacher?

"Observation more than books, experience rather than persons, are the prime educators," asserts philosopher and education reformer Amos B. Alcott, father of the noted American author, Louisa May Alcott.

This does not mean that words do not have their place. Words form a vital link in the essential chain of experiences. Learned men have labored for years accumulating knowledge that you and I can benefit. Whenever I've had a question, I've always researched it in the library or on the Internet; but whenever a question would pop into memory while reading a book, I would always attempt to prove it with my own experience. I've always been a pragmatist: if it works in my personal experience, I use it until it doesn't work any more.

I've also had a healthy curiosity about the more subtle parts of myself – my body, my thoughts, my feelings, or what psychologists call the subconscious or what religionists may call the Holy Spirit. When it comes to my physical health, I know that all of these play a part.

One day, without even thinking about education, this thought pushed its way into my memory. All the subjects I've been taught all these years have been placed in little pockets. Every class I attended was a different subject to be placed into a different pocket, seldom to be mixed together: physics in this pocket, and psychology in that one. The greatest prohibition of all is never to speak about any of these in the same breath with religion or subjects of the Spirit. When it comes to my health, I want to use any useful information no matter what subject heading my educators chose to place it under. This is especially true of religion and subjects of the Spirit.

Upon reexamining the subjects taught during my formal education, I gradually began to see connections. As I explored these connections, many concepts that confused me in my early years suddenly became clear. For example, in high school, when I saw the term X-squared in algebra class, I knew that it meant the multiplication of X by itself. However, it was never explained to me that, in practical terms, it represented the area of a square room or carpet. As I examined each of these early subjects, and began to see at least one connection among all of them, many concepts that were cloudy suddenly became clear. In subsequent chapters I will build bridges among many of the sciences, psychology and our religious beliefs, because I am now convinced that they are inseparable.

Pythagoras

The first time I heard the name Pythagoras was in my high school Trigonometry course. That was when I had to memorize the Pythagorean Theorem: $a^2+b^2=c^2$. In more recent years, the name Pythagoras has persistently resurfaced. I was reading a text that called his celebrated theorem one of the most important discoveries in the history of mathematics. An entire system of mathematics has been structured around this theorem. I became fascinated with this man. I decided to dig further.

Pythagoras was born in Samos, Greece in 582 BC and in 538 moved to Croton, Southern Italy. He eventually established the Order of Pythagoreans in 500 BC. A rebellion broke out against the order and scattered his followers far and wide. Unconventional teachings about philosophy, psychology, science and medicine were suppressed in those times, even as they are today. He traveled extensively thereafter, introducing philosophy as a way of life.

Unlike the educational methods today, Pythagoras did not place each subject in a different pocket. He really only taught one subject that included: mathematics, music, physics, chemistry, biology, astronomy, religion, and the many related subjects. What link could he possibly find among such a broad and diverse array of subjects?

Pythagorean mathematics of nature stressed that all things consist of numbers, literally. In his *Harmony of the Spheres* those numbers took on the nature of cycles and vibrations. Pythagoras understood, perhaps better than anyone of his time or since, the effect of vibration on nature, on our health, and on our state of consciousness. Mathematical systems that he established still hold up in today's modern world.

The Unity of all Life - Scientists have shown quite conclusively that the things we can see and touch in our physical world, are made of the same stuff: molecules constructed from atoms. What about the more personal experiences in our lives: our thoughts, our feelings, our dreams, our imagination, our visions for the future? What influence do they have on whether we are rich or poor, happy or sad, healthy or unhealthy?

We might wonder how the structure that scientists have built for our physical world could ever be in unity with those more subtle parts of ourselves. This is the question we must answer if we ever hope to dissolve the "root cause" of our illness. To heal the root cause of illness we must target a specific illness, such as cancer, heart disease, influenza, and link it directly to what we've been thinking, feeling, dreaming, and imagining what we would like to have in our future.

Disease as a Symbol or Metaphor

Tom Trowbridge, in his book, *The Hidden Meaning of Illness*, wrote that "Illnesses have meaning in the same way that dreams have meaning. Like symbols in our dreams, our illnesses are messages from our psyche – the inner self – which can be interpreted and understood. But our illnesses are not the problem. They are only symptoms or symbols of the real problem. The real problem is spiritual, an imbalance or distortion in our thinking, attitudes and feelings."

Jesus said it in this way: "There is nothing outside a man that, entering into him, can defile him; but the things that come out of a man, these are what defile a man." Again he said, "Out of the abundance of the heart, the mouth speaks." Or "We reap what we sow." These same thoughts may also be found in the writings of the ancient religion of Judea and other religious scriptures.

The Cabala - "This is one of the greatest principles ever given in the field of thought," wrote Paul Twitchell in his master work,

<u>The Flute of God</u>. He was commenting on an obscure spiritual law of Correspondence, "as above, so below," found in the *Cabala*, the mystical teaching of the ancient religion of Judea. According to Paul Twitchell, our experiences in this physical world (below) are merely reflections of realities in the more subtle spiritual realms (above). The symbol of Judaism itself reflects this profound teaching. It consists of two equilateral triangles, one that points upward and one that points downward to form the star of Israel.

"As above, so below," the second Hermetic Principle, is found in the *Kybalion*, a part of the *Cabala*. This book contains the writings of Hermes Trismegistus, who is believed to have dwelt in Egypt in the days of Abraham (of Biblical fame). Hermes, sometimes called "The Great," "The Master of Masters and scribe of the gods," was said to be a teacher of the *Old Testament's* Abraham. "As above, so below" reveals the secret to understanding the more subtle communications of life: the deeper meaning of the parables of Jesus, the language of dreams, the deeper understanding of classic literature and art, as well as the "root" cause of illness. Objects or symbols in the physical world all have their parallels in the world of ideas and spirit.

Food, for example, represents that which we eat to sustain the physical body. We have also heard the expression: "food for thought," "food for soul," or "You're just feeding your emotions." In everyday language we often use the symbols around us to represent some higher aspect of our reality. Here are some other examples: She's as sly as a FOX. He eats like a PIG. They work him like a HORSE. She was overcome by WAVES of emotion. That's a MEATY problem. I'll have to CHEW on that idea a while.

We also may apply this idea to the two states of consciousness found within ourselves. As a human being, we are made up of a higher (emotional, mental, & spiritual) self, and a lower (physical) self. We might further equate "above" to our higher nature and "below" to our lower nature. Let us assume that

"Above" represents our thoughts, our emotions, and our true self, Soul, and that "below", represents our physical body.

We might further state that all of the symbols in our life below: tables, chairs, houses, and human conditions, began with a thought. Would it not be interesting if the things we see around us and the feelings we experience within us, are a mere reflection of the original mental/emotional experience that has already taken place at that higher level of our awareness "above."

CHAPTER FOURTEEN

Digging Up Roots - Part II

How do we know when our house or garden plants are sick? We only know when they are sick by observing the plant above the ground. Are the leaves a rich green color or are they wilting, turning yellow, purple, or gray? Is the soil dry or standing in water? Are they getting enough sunshine?

In many ways, we humans are like plants. We know we are ill by looking for signs: a rash on the skin, a lump on the breast or a cracking of the nails. Unlike plants, we know when we have a pain in our side, suffer from fatigue, or have impaired sight or hearing. When any of these symptoms occur, most of us will consult a physician, but many of us will avoid them. Maybe, like many today, we can't afford the treatment. Or maybe we're afraid of what examination might reveal. Who has made the best decision? This answer might surprise you. A recent study in the JAMA (Journal of the American Medical Association) reported that condemned cancer patients who declined treatment using chemotherapy or radiation lived longer than those who took the treatment. This and other studies have led me to question the practices of family physicians in general.

Family Physicians

In a 1999 report, the Institute of Medicine estimated that as many as 98,000 Americans die every year because of medical errors. The Journal of the American Medical Association

(JAMA) published much more serious statistics. This article in the Journal of the American Medical Association (JAMA) is the best article I have ever seen written in the published literature documenting the tragedy of the traditional medical paradigm.

This information is a follow-up of the Institute of Medicine report which hit the papers in December several years ago, but the data was hard to reference as it was not in peer-reviewed journal. Now it is published in JAMA which is the most widely circulated medical periodical in the world. The author is Dr. Barbara Starfield of the Johns Hopkins School of Hygiene and Public Health and she describes how the US health care system may contribute to poor health.

ALL THESE ARE DEATHS PER YEAR:
* 12,000 -- Unnecessary surgery
* 7,000 -- Medication errors in hospitals
* 20,000 -- Other errors in hospitals
* 80,000 -- Infections in hospitals
* 106,000 -- Non-error, negative effects of drugs

These numbers total 250,000 deaths per year from iatrogenic causes. What does the word iatrogenic mean? This term is defined as induced in a patient by a physician's activity, manner, or therapy. Used especially of a complication of treatment.

If the higher estimates are used, the deaths due to iatrogenic causes would range from 230,000 to 284,000. In any case, 225,000 deaths per year constitute the third leading cause of death in the United States, after deaths from heart disease and cancer. Even if these figures are overestimated, there is a wide margin between these numbers of deaths and the next leading cause of death (cerebrovascular disease).

Another analysis concluded that between 4% and 18% of consecutive patients experience negative effects in outpatient settings, with:
* 116 million extra physician visits
* 77 million extra prescriptions
* 17 million emergency department visits

- 8 million hospitalizations
- 3 million long-term admissions
- 199,000 additional deaths
- $77 billion in extra costs

The high cost of the health care system is considered to be a deficit, but seems to be tolerated under the assumption that better health results from more expensive care. However, evidence from a few studies indicates that as many as 20% to 30% of patients receive inappropriate care. An estimated 44,000 to 98,000 among them die each year as a result of medical errors.

This might be tolerated if it resulted in better health, but does it? Of 13 countries in a recent comparison among the more advanced populations, the United States ranks an average of 12th (second from the bottom) for 16 available health indicators. More specifically, the ranking of the US on several indicators was:

- 13th (last) for low-birth-weight percentages
- 13th for neonatal mortality and infant mortality overall
- 11th for post=neonatal mortality
- 13th for years of potential life lost (excluding external causes)
- 11th for life expectancy at 1 year for females, 12th for males
- 10th for life expectancy at 15 years for females, 12th for males
- 10th for life expectancy at 40 years for females, 9th for males
- 7th for life expectancy at 65 years for females, 7th for males
- 3rd for life expectancy at 80 years for females, 3rd for males
- 10th for age-adjusted mortality

The poor performance of the US was recently confirmed by a World Health Organization study, which used different data and ranked the United States as 15th among 25 industrialized countries.

There is a perception that the American public "behaves badly" by smoking, drinking, and perpetrating violence." However the data does not support this assertion.

- The proportion of females who smoke ranges from 14% in Japan to 41% in Denmark; in the United States, it is 24% (fifth best). For males, the range is from 26% in Sweden to 61% in Japan; it is 28% in the United States (third best).
- The US ranks fifth best for alcoholic beverage consumption.
- The US has relatively low consumption of animal fats --fifth lowest in men aged 55-64 years in 20 industrialized countries, and the third lowest mean cholesterol concentrations among men aged 50 to 70 years among 13 industrialized countries.

These estimates of death due to error are lower than those in a recent Institutes of Medicine report, and if the higher estimates are used, the deaths due to iatrogenic causes would range from 230,000 to 284,000.

Even at the lower estimate of 225,000 deaths per year, this constitutes the third leading cause of death in the US, following heart disease and cancer.

Lack of technology is certainly not a contributing factor to the US's low ranking.

- Among 29 countries, the United States is second only to Japan in the availability of magnetic resonance imaging units and computed tomography scanners per million population. 17
- Japan, however, ranks highest on health, whereas the US ranks among the lowest.
- It is possible that the high use of technology in Japan is limited to diagnostic technology not matched by high rates of treatment, whereas in the US, high use of diagnostic technology may be linked to more treatment.

- Supporting this possibility are data showing that the number of employees per bed (full-time equivalents) in the United States is highest among the countries ranked, whereas they are very low in Japan, far lower than can be accounted for by the common practice of having family members rather than hospital staff provide the amenities of hospital care.

Source of the above material:

Journal American Medical Association, July26, 2000; 284:483-5

(http://www.mercola.com/2000/jul/30/doctors death.htm)

A study by the National Council on Patient Information and Education showed that at least 125,000 people each year die from prescription drugs their doctors never should have given them because they had pre-existing conditions that are clearly contraindicated in the drugs' packaging. Many people naturally trust their doctors and pharmacists to prevent these kinds of problems. Other studies have shown that, more than ever, each of us has to be our own watchdog.

So what should a person do?

I will assume from the start that we are all interested in discovering and resolving the "root cause of our illnesses," and I know from direct experience that doctors are never trained to diagnose the "root cause of illness." The modern allopathic doctor is trained to assign names to symptoms (i.e., cancer, Lupus or MS), and then prescribe a "drug" that will attempt to suppress them. More often than not, the cure will be as bad or worse than the disease.

Taking Responsibility

In previous chapters, I've shared with you a few physical actions we can take to improve our health considerably. These include: drinking 8-10 glasses of pure water daily, special exercise routines, diet, supplements, create healthy electromagnetic environment, and, still more importantly, attitude.

I've learned over the years that in order to motivate myself to take actions that will change my life for the better, I must always convince my mind that it's worth pursuing. Even though I may have a powerful intuitive feeling that I must change my diet, go to a health practitioner, or practice daily exercise, etc., I must first convince my mind in a logical, step-by-step process how any action will benefit the total human system.

We must always remember that "mind" does not like change. It likes the groove that it's stuck in, no matter how destructive it may be. This is the primary reason for these chapters on *Digging Up Roots*. I plan to build step-by-step links from symptom to "root cause" so the mind can understand. Our minds understand cause and effect relationships. The symptom is only the "effect" of a much deeper, hidden chain of events that "caused" the symptom.

The Unity of all Life

Earlier I mentioned the way our society tends to place the different parts of our universe into little pockets: Physics in one pocket, Medicine in that pocket, and psychology in another. The greatest prohibition of all is never to speak about any of these in the same breath with religion or subjects of the Spirit. If we wish to truly understand why we get sick and how we can be healthy, we must first reject these ideas.

Scientists have shown quite conclusively that the things we can see and touch in our physical world, are made of the same stuff: molecules constructed from atoms. But what we must also consider are the more personal experiences in our lives: our thoughts, our feelings, our dreams, our imagination, our visions for the future. Many of our greatest philosophers -- Pythagoras, Plato, Aristotle – wrote about the profound influence that the more subtle parts of us have on whether we are rich or poor, happy or sad, healthy or unhealthy?

I also remember the teachings of Jesus who taught that it is not unwashed hands that defile a man, but every word that comes out of his mouth, for it is in the abundance of the heart that the mouth speaks.

We might wonder how the structure that scientists have built for our physical world could ever be in unity with those more subtle parts of ourselves. This is the question we must answer if we ever hope to understand the root cause of our illness. To heal the root cause of illness we must begin at the most basic part of ourselves: atoms, cells, and their energy.

Back to the Basics

We all know about the basic unit of life. What better place to begin our study of health than with the basic unit of life, the atom. Every organ in our bodies consists of cells constructed of molecules which are built from atoms.

When we look at the picture of the atom that scientists have provided us we see high energy electrons orbiting clusters of neutrons and protons. Every organ in our bodies is constructed from these high energy units. Why do we go through periods of fatigue when we know that trillions of these amazing entities are generating so much energy? Why is that energy not available to us for our day-to-day activities?

Energy

Energy is defined as the capacity to do work. The atom has built within it two kinds of energy: potential energy and kinetic energy. The potential energy of the atom is that energy which bonds the protons and neutrons together at the center of the atom. This is the energy that is released when the atom is split apart. Kinetic Energy is the energy that sustains the motion of the electrons in their orbit around the atom. What happens to this energy when we become sick?

Chapter Fifteen.

Digging Up Roots - Part III

The common dilemma most scientists face is their inability to explain the many phenomena they have observed while continuing wholehearted support of the popular quantum physics theories. Quantum physics is based on the traditional model of the atom that we all know consisting of a proton/ neutron nucleus with orbiting electrons. Everything in our universe appears to be constructed of these "atoms." What have scientists discovered that causes this model to come into question?

The Atom

Please keep in mind while reading this discourse that the performance of the atoms in our bodies is what affects our health. What happens to these atoms when we get sick will become clear as this series proceeds.

Atomic scientists have already shown decades ago that when you can break up the atom into its smallest components, you end up with only energy. Atomic particles that appeared to be solid, when split apart, are really only energy.

When we visualize an electron, for example, we think of a tiny electrically charged sphere, but scientists have shown that it actually has no dimensions at all. What we could visualize is an electromagnetic energy field of varying strength and polarity that surrounds the nucleus of the atom instead of electrons. To place this phenomenon in human terms, the electromagnetic energy field of the atom could very well be called the aura of the atom. Since everything in our world is constructed of atoms, then everything in our world also has an energy field or aura.

The energy of the atom is perpetual. Every atom in our bodies seems to have unlimited supplies of energy. How is this possible? Such a concept would seem to violate every acceptable law of physics. What I am going to propose in the following paragraphs may seem like a giant leap over the beliefs of many who read this material. But the following ideas do seem logical to many based on the research of many broadminded scientists as well as churchmen.

The Energy Source

In an earlier chapter, we discussed the way most of us have been educated. Every class we attended was placed into a different pocket, seldom to be mixed together: physics in this pocket, and psychology in that one. But the greatest prohibition of all is never to speak about any of these sciences in the same breath with religion or subjects of the Spirit. This practice has created serious roadblocks in the paths of many physical scientists -- with a few exceptions. A few scientists, however, have refused to be blocked in that way.

Physicist David Bohm, a University of London physicist and protégé' of Albert Einstein, implied in his masterwork, entitled Holomovement, that a long list of the laws of physics appear to be a mere reflection of the laws of Spirit and psychology. Bohm astounded the physicist community with the pronouncement that everything in the universe is a part of a gigantic, ever evolving space-time continuum (space and time considered together as one entity).

Bohm further concluded that dividing our world into animal and mineral, organic and inorganic also makes no sense. Matter that we consider dead or inorganic still has energy, only in a different form. This idea has already been accepted under the "Conservation of energy" law which states that "energy can be neither created nor destroyed but merely transformed into another state."

Bohm has also shown that every cubic centimeter of empty space possesses the energy of the whole, even in a vacuum. The conclusion we finally arrive at is that our world is a mass of powerful, intelligent atoms with varying frequencies and polarities. Interestingly, many of Bohm's colleagues consider this theory highly credible.

A memory from my past flashed across my mind when I first read about Bohm's pronouncement that every cubic centimeter in our universe possesses the energy of the whole,. I recalled memorizing passages as a child in the early elementary grades. They were questions and answers from the Catechism of Christian Doctrine (Kincade's Baltimore Series of Catechisms - No.2). I pulled the book from my library shelf and read: "Who is God? God is the creator of heaven and earth and all things. Where is God? **God is everywhere**. What is man? Man is a creature composed of body and Soul, and made in the image and likeness of God. Is this likeness in the body or in the Soul? This likeness is chiefly in the Soul.

Can we see the parallel between "God is everywhere" and Bohm's pronouncement that every centimeter has the power of the whole. Every religion I have studied believes that "God is Omnipotent, Omniscient, and Omnipresent." In all good conscience, how can scientists say that God is everywhere, except in the physical world?"

If an all-wise, all-powerful God is everywhere, then Bohm's implication that every atom possesses the energy of the whole, seems to be in perfect harmony with this Christian Doctrine and the beliefs of many other religions. This could also mean that every atom in our bodies is a part of God possessing the wisdom and the power of God.

It is perfectly understandable that many will find such a belief difficult to accept. However, one thing we do know is that every cell in our body has energy and intelligence. Each cell in our body knows its own function as well as the function of every other cell in the body. Such intelligence is built into the DNA of every cell. The medical profession knows it, otherwise how could the body function so well for so many years considering the abuse that we, as well as doctors, shower upon it.

It's not necessary, however, that anyone believe these outrageous proposals in order to understand the "Root Cause of Illness." But immediate questions arise -- for example: If I have all this power and wisdom dwelling in my own body, why do I get sick? If there is so much power and wisdom in every centimeter of the universe, why do we have polluted air, water and food? Why don't we have a perfect world? – All good questions that will be addressed.

In the meantime let us accept what science has demonstrated. 1. The basic structural unit of our body is the atom. 2. Each atom is endowed with dynamic energy and intelligence.

The Nature of Energy

In Physics, energy is defined as "The capacity to do work." Physics has placed energy into two broad categories: Potential energy and Kinetic energy. Energy in motion is called kinetic. Energy is potential by nature of its position or its physical nature. The best example of these two types of energy may be seen where man has dammed up a river to produce electricity. The dam converts the kinetic energy of the river into potential energy in a reservoir. The potential energy of the water in the reservoir is then converted back to kinetic energy as it is fed through turbines to create electricity.

Our world is filled with both of these types of energy. Kinetic energy might be considered manifested energy that we can see, feel and touch. Potential energy may found in outer space and in the subtle worlds of mind, feelings, and Spirit.

Scientists call the unmanifested, potential energy in outer space: Ether, Vril, or Orgone. The popular science fiction epic, *Star Wars*, has called it "The Force." A variety of religions have called it Prana, Chi, ECK, or the Holy Spirit.

Now the question becomes: What causes this unmanifested, potential energy to become manifested Kinetic energy? Here, again forward thinking physicists have shown the way.

Several physicists have shown that an electron can register a single discrete point on a photographic plate clearly revealing that the electron can take on the nature of a particle. The electron also seems to have the ability to manifest as simply a bundle of energy (i.e. photon or quantum of energy). It seems that all subatomic particles can change from particles to waves and back to particles again. So what causes this to happen?

Physicists have chosen to call this atomic phenomenon with its dual nature, **quanta**, and that this is the stuff that our universe (and our bodies) is structured from. A still more astounding discovery about quanta is that it appears to be a particle only when it is being observed. Renowned Danish physicist, Niels Bohr proved that the atom's quanta become particles only in the presence of an observer; otherwise it is an unmanifested wave of energy. Most scientists are satisfied that Niels Bohr's conclusions are correct.

The research of David Bohm paralleled that of Niels Bohr. Bohm began to wonder how electrons behave if they were part of a mass of electrons (called plasma by scientists). Bohm discovered that single electrons ceased their random behavior and began to conform to the group's behavior just like a flock of birds or a swarm of bees might do. Electrons in a group seemed to take on the identity of the group seeming to act as a single entity, even to the extent that it took on the organic quality of reproducing itself while being observed. Bohm actually got the impression that it was alive.

Bohm's work with plasma lead him to conclude that the true nature of matter is not individual electrons acting alone, but rather they are a part of an integrated system purposefully acting toward a single objective. He concluded that every part of space is equal to all other parts of space and that no part is separate from any other part. Bohm concluded that the way an observer interacts with any group of quantum, determines the form that this mass will take. He also observed that constant interaction can produce constant change.

Are we now beginning to understand what science has proven here? Physicists have actually proven that we can influence our physical world through our thoughts – and this includes our own bodies? This idea originated from two of the World's most respected scientists: Physicist, David Bohm and Karl Pribram, a neurophysiologist at Stanford University. Using completely different and separate approaches, both men arrived at this same conclusion.

The work of these forward-thinking scientists has shown that it takes the attention of a human to <u>manifest and influence</u> the movement of atoms no matter where they are: in outer space, in our environment, or in our own bodies. All of the facts discovered by our physicists have also been demonstrated frequently in psychosomatic medicine, and alternative approaches to health care.

Initiating Change

In order to accept these powerful laws as a part of our beliefs requires a major change of viewpoint for most of us. We must give up our old ways of thinking and replace them with thought patterns more in unity with spiritual laws and the laws of physics.

David Bohm has proven that our thoughts do influence the movement of atoms. If we think only beneficial thoughts about our bodies, the atoms will come into line with our creative thinking. We help an illness to survive only by giving it our thought energy. Without our thought energy, our illness cannot survive.

Why we get sick

We can attribute our ills to many things: bad diet, water, air, food, electronic pollution, germs, or parasites, etc. These surely have their effect. From all we know today about how our thoughts can affect atoms, I would be naive to think that my thoughts could not be a major cause of my illness?

If I have all this power and wisdom dwelling in my own body, why do I get sick? If there is so much power and wisdom in every centimeter of the universe, why do we have polluted air, water and food? Why don't we have a perfect world? These will be questions for our next chapter.

CHAPTER SIXTEEN.

Digging Up Roots - Part IV

Pythagoras and his Mystery School

The great Greek Master Pythagoras, who lived in the sixth century BC, taught that all things consist of numbers, literally. In his *Harmony of the Spheres* those numbers took on the nature of cycles and vibrations. He is the originator of the mathematical system for calculating wavelengths and frequencies of vibrations - Trigonometry. Many of us will remember the basic formula for this system, the Pythagorean Theorem ($a^2+b^2=c^2$). Pythagoras understood, perhaps better than anyone of his time or since, the effect of vibration on the health and consciousness of humans. Mathematical systems that he established in the sixth century BC still hold up in today's modern world. Many scientists today call Pythagoras the greatest mathematician of all time.

The Nature of Vibrations

Every atom and every thing in our universe radiates energy, and all radiated energy is vibratory in nature. Basically, this means that the power or strength of the energy varies in a regular periodic way. The sciences conveniently represent vibration in the graphic form using the sine curve as seen in the figure below. Each sine wave shows two of the components of vibratory radiation: wavelength, and amplitude (strength). In this figure wavelength (one cycle) is represented by the Greek symbol Lambda (λ) and amplitude is represented by the height of the curve. A third component, frequency is represented by the number of cycles that occur in one period of time (seconds, hours, days, years). We will deal with cycles-per-second in this study.

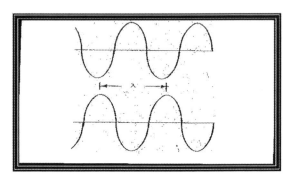

Measuring Frequency

Frequencies are measured in cycles, vibrations, or pulses per second -- often called Hertz. The Hertz is usually the term used when computer scientists want to measure the time it takes for one computer instruction cycle to occur. Everything in nature vibrates and, therefore, has a frequency. Audible Sound, for example, vibrates the air at 15 to 20,000 Hertz. Visible light has a frequency of $3x10^9$ to $3x10^7$ Hertz. X-rays have a frequency of $3x10^{15}$ to $3x10^9$ Hertz.

According to scientist Dr. Hulda Clark, the average frequency of a human body can range between 1,562,000 and 9,457,000 Hertz, insects between 1,000,000 and 1,500,000 Hertz, viruses, bacteria, and parasites between 290,000 and 470,000 Hertz. She has catalogued hundreds of our bodily invaders. She has also discovered how to destroy them by exposing them to specific electrical frequencies and polarities that are intolerable to the organisms, but do not have adverse effects on human cells. Drugs and herbal formulas with the proper frequencies and polarities have also been designed to destroy these organisms.

Polarity is the Key

In layman's terms polarity simply means opposite, as in light and dark, good and bad, right and wrong. In physics, polarity is the quality of having opposite magnetic poles as in north and south, positive and negative. In earlier chapters I have written about the "Right hand Rule" that physicists use to define the polarity of an energy field. Whenever you have a flow of electricity (electrons) through a medium (e.g., an electrical wire, your body or mine, or any atom in the universe) you will always have a field of electromagnetic energy surrounding it.

The reverse of this rule is also true. Whenever you find an energy field around anything, it is certain that a dynamic energy is passing through it.

It is already an accepted fact that we humans are surrounded by an energy field called our aura. If the force of our field (aura) is clockwise, then, according to the "Right Hand Rule," our energy is entering our bodies at the top of our head and flowing downward. Therefore, our polarity is considered positive. If the force of our energy field is counterclockwise, then the originating energy is entering the body near the base of the spine and our polarity is considered negative. Everything in our universe has either positive or negative polarity. Let's say that the top sine curve in the above figure is considered positive and the bottom sine curve is considered negative. These curves have opposite polarities because when the one curve is curving up the other is curving down. If we were to add these two curves together mathematically, the one would cancel the other and the result would be zero energy. This is the secret of healing remedies like herbs, vitamins, minerals, Miracle-II, or any energy of the proper frequency and amplitude.

CHAPTER SEVENTEEN.

Digging Up Roots - Part V

In her research, Professor Laura Kubzansky, from the Harvard School of Public Health, discovered that optimism lowers the risk of heart disease in older men, while pessimism and hopelessness increase the possibility of heart disease.

In the January 27, 2004 issue of *Time* magazine (UK Version) health reporter Kate Rew wrote an article entitled *Mind Over Matter.*
(*http://www.timesonline.co.uk/article/0,,8123-978120,00. html*) which stated that:

Positive thought can be as effective as drugs in beating disease, studies show.

Preventative medicine may soon mean more than just monitoring your vegetable intake and exercise levels, and include how many negative thoughts go through your head in a day.

'There is a growing body of evidence to suggest that a patient's beliefs and hopes affect their prognosis.

One of the major contributors to maintaining health and removing disease is the attitude of the patient ,says Professor Oakley Ray, a psychologist from Vanderbilt University in Tennessee. Professor Ray reviewed 100 years of research on psychology and disease for a paper published in *American Psychologist*, and he concluded that; 'words can have the same effect as drugs: thinking optimistically can change your whole biology.

There is strong evidence that patients with heart disease who feel hopeless about their condition do worse,' says Professor Alan Steptoe, a psychologist at University College London, 'but whether this attitude can be changed is still an open question.'

Is it really impossible to alter, change or even replace our attitude with something that is more agreeable to us? Is it possible for us to change our attitude toward our health, toward our situations in life, our family, our job, our financial situation? If we could change our attitude, why would we want to change it, what would we change it to, and how would we go about changing it?

Why Change Our Attitude?

Our attitude is a mental state that involves how our mind will react under specific situations. Our attitude depends on what we believe, and how we feel emotionally about life and our experiences in life. Our attitude involves the values that we place on objects and people in our lives. Our attitudes define how we will react, emotionally or physically, while surrounded by pressures that we can see, as well as, those inner pressures that we cannot see or even understand.

As I look back on my growing-up years at home I remember only happy, contented attitudes. Then I reached the age of six and the Educational Institutional Matrix sank its jaws into my consciousness. I hated most of my 12 years of schooling. My attitude toward my formal education was the direct opposite of my home life. Where did those attitudes come from? Attitudes are like habits—grooves or engrams impressed on the mind through repeated past experiences. In my early life, I had no time to build such strongly felt attitudes. These had to be attitudes built up through many past lifetimes.

As I look at most of my attitudes today, I cannot really say why I have any of them. I don't know why I love spinach and dislike strawberries; why I prefer listening to classical music, but dislike most operas; why I prefer quiet conversation with a friend to riding the roller coaster at amusement park.

I attribute today's attitudes to experiences I had in other lifetimes. I believe all of my strongly held attitudes were formed in other lifetimes. I don't necessarily want to change all of my attitudes if they cause me no discomfort. However, I do have attitudes that call up painful emotions. These are the one's that I do wish to change, and these are the attitudes that cause me to react in a negative or destructive manner. Negative or destructive emotions are not only painful when I experience them, but, as I now know, they are also destroying my health.

So, if anyone ever asked me: "why would I want to change my attitude? I would answer: "Because I want to feel good and live a longer, healthier, happier, and have a higher quality of life.

Which Attitudes Should I Change?

Once I decided to change my attitudes, I had to decide what it was that I wanted to change. I sat down and made a list of the feelings that I occasionally have that I don't particularly enjoy. Here are a few of the more common ones: anger, fear, stress, depression, worry, excessive pride, uncontrolled lust, and unnecessary attachments.

When I was in my youth, I can recall experiencing raw out-of-control anger. Through the use of my inner resources, I have, fortunately, removed that kind of anger from my life. Unfortunately, impatience, a lesser form of anger, has still retained its grip. I get impatient at red traffic lights; I get impatient waiting in doctor's or dentist's office; I get impatient with rude and incompetent drivers on the highway; I get impatient with my friends when they aren't listening when I speak, and many others. All of these are not only destructive to my health, but, more importantly, to my wellbeing. They also retard my spiritual development.

Fear has been called "the most destructive emotion" of all human experiences. A few years ago, I decided to make a list of the things that I fear? I could barely fit them all on one page. Here are just a few: fear of death, fear of illness, fear of pain, fear of being wrong, fear of criticism, fear of being mugged, fear of break-ins, fear of heights, fear of being alone, and, my worst fear of all, fear of speaking before a group of more than one. In a recent pole, "fear of public speaking" was the greatest fear on most people's list, even ahead of fear of death.

I've been a technician all of my professional life, but I knew that eventually I would reach my pinnacle as a technician and be forced into a supervisory position. I finally did find myself in a position of leadership where I would have to speak in front of groups. I knew I had to somehow dissolve that nemesis of fear. I contemplated the problem and posed the question to my inner guide (we all have one): "How can I rid myself of my fears?"

Getting Rid of Fear

It is a simple case of the law that states - what you hold in your consciousness and give energy to in the form of emotion and feeling does polarize your energetic field and draws to you that which you do fear most. Fear is one of the key elements by which the heart is kept closed, and the intuition, love, and power from above being heard. And the power of love and of the heart, and the wisdom and truth that is found there, is the greatest threat of all to those who seek by power and fear to maintain what they have achieved. Surrender truly is the key to surpassing the fear that grips the heart and is generated by the mind. Through surrender and vigilance and discipline and trust will the heart be truly opened and the goal be attained and realized. (The Way of Truth Eternal IV by Michael Owens)

The heart center is the more subtle energy center behind that part of us known as the Thymus Gland located just above the heart. Interestingly, the heart has perennially been associated with the virtue of Love and compassion (e.g. "She has a kind heart," "Have a heart!" and "He's hard-hearted.").

How do I open a heart center that is closed? The only answer that came to me was to place my attention at the heart center during my contemplative exercises that I do every morning. I began to place my attention there during my contemplations while I sang inwardly an ancient name for God, HU. I sing it, aloud or silently, in a long drawn-out fashion like this: "HUUuuuuuuu."

I continued this practice for about a month without much success; nevertheless, I have learned that one of the more important, but seldom mentioned, virtues in life is persistence. "Patience and Perseverance have a magical effect before which difficulties disappear and obstacles vanish." John Quincy Adams

I did continue the exercise into the second month. After another week of the month, I began to sense a tingling sensation around the heart center. Another week passed and I felt a love sensation around the center. As I continued the exercise, the love grew stronger. By the end of the month the love was almost overwhelming. It wasn't love **for** anybody or anything, but just a wonderful love feeling that flowed through my whole body. My only thought was that it is God's love for me. I eventually returned to my traditional exercise placing my attention on my spiritual eye, but first making sure that love was in my heart.

In subsequent months, I realized that, one-by-one, even my worst fears miraculously began to disappear - even the fear of speaking before a group. While all these fears still do attempt to return at times, I now know the key to abolishing them. Love overcomes fear.

What Attitudes Should I Create for Myself?

I consistently want to maintain an attitude that promotes a sense of wellbeing in my life. This means that at any given time, I can honestly say the following: I feel good about myself. I feel good about my experiences with my family as well as my coworkers. I feel good about every aspect of my life - my health and my finances. Every experience in my life is a blessing.

I know there will be times when experiences might tend to upset my balance, but I must never let the effect of any of those old experiences or thoughts return. If my thoughts want to carry me into any of those earlier states—the anger, the fear, the pride—I will shift my attention to my heart center where I feel that love during my contemplations. I now know that I have all the power, the wisdom, and the love that I need to overcome any adversity.

Right now I can hear my limited mind saying to me: "Yea, right. Who do you think you are kidding? Get real." This would probably be a normal reaction for me in my early life. However, I finally discovered that these are not **my_**thoughts that I'm thinking. They come from this tool God gave me that I call my mind. I'm not my mind or my thoughts. I am a HU-man being. HU is an ancient name for God. I must always remember that I am a God-man whose abilities are unlimited.

This is the goal I've set for myself. Every minute of the day I cultivate that attitude of my new role as God-man. This is what Jesus did. "I and the Father are One." Jesus came to show our possibilities as God-men. If we want to live a life like he lived, we can do it.

Every day, I tell myself: "I am a spiritual being called Soul. I have no limitations, because, as all religions teach, 'God is everywhere,' especially in my heart." Tearing down the barriers that prevent me from realizing my full potential is now a major goal in my life.

The Power of Faith

Shortly after Mel Gibson's blockbuster film, *The Passion of the Christ,* began playing in the theatres, the NBC program Dateline broadcasted an excellent program entitled *The Power of Faith.* The program consisted of four segments: *Faith that Heals, The Servant Leader, The Physical Effects of Faith, and The Miracles of Jesus.* It will definitely be worth the time it will take to check out www.Dateline.MSNBC.Com for the full story. Here, briefly, is some of what took place.

1. The Faith that Heals - Studies have shown that belief in the ability of a higher power to heal the body is a fact. That faith gains its power when the individual takes on the attitude of

surrendering to a higher power. They made the reference to the miracles of Jesus. Whenever he healed anyone, he never took the credit himself, he always closed with *"Thy faith has made thee whole."*

A recent Gallup poll found that three in four Americans believe their lives have meaning and purpose because of their faith.

2. The Servant Leader - Robert Greenleaf has written a book *The Servant Leader* proposing that the role of any leader in a corporation is far more effective if they have an attitude of service rather than that of a dictator.

What is Servant-Leadership? Servant-Leadership is a practical philosophy which supports people who choose to serve first, and then lead as a way of expanding service to individuals and institutions. Servant-leaders may or may not hold formal leadership positions. Servant-leadership encourages collaboration, trust, foresight, listening, and the ethical use of power and empowerment.

This is the attitude that all spiritually committed people practice daily. Like Mother Theresa and others, they ask: How can I serve today?

3. The Physical Effects of Faith - Research has discovered that there is a corner of the brain that is devoted to that "sense of self" or the ego aspect of human nature. A study was conducted involving specific religious individuals whose life is God-oriented. The study showed that, while they meditated or prayed, the "Sense of Self" in every individual tested fades away to become more a part of the whole of life.

4. The Miracles of Jesus - Why did Jesus perform so many miracles? Religious authorities propose that it was not to show that he had any special power, but rather to teach the lesson that **everyone** has the power. Jesus said "I have come to show the possibilities of men." (*The Aquarian Gospel of Jesus the Christ* by Levi Dowling)

CHAPTER EIGHTEEN

Dimensions of Life - Part I
Introduction

I recently asked myself: What are the dimensions of this world I live in that impact my health, wealth, and well being? I ask this question because this is what causes me to be what I am today. I am made up of the materials of this world. My environment, what I am made from, and what I believe, determines what I become - my health, well-being and my status in the world.

I am going to assume that my environment, including myself, is made up of four components: matter, energy, space, and time. I'm going to call this MEST. I'm also going to assume that I have power over all of these elements. Within my own world I can make them what I want them to be.

I have also asked myself: What are the forces in this world that have, in the past and in the present, hindered me from using the powers that I have to change my world? One of the more important answers that came to me is "understanding." Why do I not have the understanding that I need to achieve my goals? The next few chapters will focus on improving my understanding of my world so that I may better accomplish the goals of health, wealth, and well-being.

Understanding the Matrix

When we come into this life as a physical being, a matrix of values has long previously been established for us by institutions that were set up centuries before. What do we mean by "Matrix?"

The only time I can recall ever seeing the word was while I was selecting math courses in college. One of the courses was Matrix Algebra, a method for solving a series of equations simultaneously. I couldn't see the connection between Matrix Algebra and the popular *Matrix* movie, so I decided to do some research using what has become my indispensable tool, the Internet.

I discovered that a Matrix can take on many different forms. A matrix can be applied in much broader terms than the mathematical matrix. It can be viewed simply as a group of related items arranged in a format of columns and rows.

Mathematicians use Matrices (plural of Matrix) to solve simultaneous equations. In order to solve the three equations below simultaneously, for example, a mathematician might build the three matrices below them and perform a few simple arithmetic operations to arrive at a solution.

The head of a family might wish to build a matrix (or table) of household expenses.

The Spreadsheet is a software package that is designed specifically for the purpose of building different matrices. A corporate accountant will use them to manage the income and expenses of a company. A simple matrix might look like this.

Year Income Expense Profit
2001 | 16,000 | 15,000 | 1000
2002 | 18,000 | 16,000 | 2000

The Matrix movie, I've concluded, has none of the traditional forms of Matrices illustrated above. Therefore, it can not possibly be the theme of the movie. In *The Matrix* we seem to be dealing with the human state of consciousness that has enslaved mass populations. I felt that the message coming from Neo's computer, as well as the dialogue of Morpheus, was referring to that state of consciousness. Here is a bit of dialogue from *The Matrix* Movie:

Neo's Computer: "Wake up, Neo. The Matrix has you."
Morpheus: "I am trying to free your mind Neo."

This tells me that I, like Neo, have permitted myself to be trapped in a Matrix of values that spell stagnate growth. More specifically, my attitudes, my beliefs, and all those deep mental grooves, or habits that define my current state of consciousness are counterproductive to my personal and spiritual growth. They seem to stem from my willingness to give up my responsibility for so many aspects of my life that I have lost control of it by submitting to an "Institutional Matrix" of values. My submission to whatever society and its institutions have built for me through centuries of my existence caused me to become lazy and apathetic. As I look back on my life, I begin to see that the people and institutions that have built my current state of consciousness are many. A few of them were portrayed in the blockbuster motion picture, *The Matrix*, but two vital pieces were missing from the movie's matrix puzzle:

1. A detailed description of the institutions whose purpose is to trap me and hold me in the Matrix, and

2. A step-by-step procedure that I can follow that will guide me out of the matrix without the use of a computer, but rather through my own natural faculties as a physical, mental, spiritual being. (The book *My Journey Through the Matrix* is currently being prepared for publication.)

To find a path out of the Matrix I must first develop a graphic image of what this matrix looks like. Clearly to build a matrix capable of molding my attitudes, beliefs, and mental patterns must consist of the institutions currently in place worldwide that existed long before I ever came into this life. The matrix below reflects those institutions that I believe have entrapped me as well as Neo and probably mass populations worldwide:

Institutions	Information	Beliefs	Habits
Family	A	B	C
Education	D	E	F
Churches	G	H	I
Governments	J	K	L
Financial	M	N	O
Health Care	P	Q	R
Industrial Complex	S	T	U
Mass Media	V	W	X

The Matrix of letters (above) might represent any number of things, from a percentage of influence exerted on my attitudes and beliefs, to a specific list of values instilled in my consciousness. Above are the institutions that I have permitted to entrap me. The laws laid down for living in this Matrix are many and the consequences of violating them are harsh. This institutional Matrix has entrapped me for eons, but it is now time to be free. The first step toward freedom is understanding the enemy but, even more importantly, we must understand the tools we need to free ourselves from this matrix that has entrapped us.

Energy

Energy, the second component of the MEST quadrangle, is the result of vibration that we discussed earlier. Energy is what sustains me in these lower worlds: physical energy, mental energy, emotional energy, and spiritual energy. I must accept total responsibility for the application of all of these vibrations. I created them, made them, and brought them into manifested reality by my reactions to the world around and within me. This means I must take full responsibility for the current state of my health, wealth, and well being. It's not always easy to admit, but we have willingly surrendered responsibility to society's Institutional Matrix.

"Until you understand that nothing can happen to you, nothing can ever come to you or be kept from you except in accordance with the state of your consciousness, you do not have the key to life." (*The Flute of God* by Paul Twitchell)

Once I've decided, like Neo (of *The Matrix* Movie), to take back my life from the Institutional Matrix I relieve myself of the burden of finding someone else to blame for my problems. As Neo has shown, the Institutional Matrix does not like to loose its slaves because the loss of each slave weakens the Matrix.

As we have shown earlier, we have access to unlimited energy and wisdom. So with the proper use of thought energy, emotional energy, and spiritual energy we have the keys to our freedom and nothing can stop us. To succeed, we fill our consciousness with the right thoughts, the right attitudes, right action, and the love of life.

Polarity

Polarity is the law of the opposites where light is opposite of dark, sound is opposite to silence, and love is opposite to hate. The Law of Polarity states that every phenomenon in these worlds is the result of combining of two forces, positive and negative, plus the third force that is the balancing of the two.

In 1956, a lady by the name of Ethyl Starbard was a very sick woman. She had an intolerance of many pollutants found in the fresh fruits and vegetables she was eating. When the fruit was exposed to the proper energy fields, the pollution was no longer present.

According to Ethyl Starbard, the results of this experiment was due to the polarity of atomic vibration that determines whether it will be harmful (disharmonious) or beneficial (harmonious) to humans. When the body is injured, or becomes ill, the energy flows counter-clockwise. The exposure of injured tissue to atoms vibrating in a clockwise direction, as in natural radiation, will polarize (reverse polarity from negative to positive) the injured tissue to return to normal. Predatory insects, on the other hand, have atoms vibrating in a counter-clockwise direction and find it intolerable when exposed to a clockwise flow of atoms.

Harmony

Harmony is a state of agreement or proportion between or among the vibrations of various states, objects, or materials. In the world of physics and vibration, perfect harmony means that the vibration of one object or condition is precisely equal to another. In our physical world this usually means that the one vibration enhances the other. A lack of harmony, on the other hand, usually means that the one vibration is destructive to the other.

In the 1940's Dr. Royal R. Rife, a research scientist experimenting with the effects of electromagnetic vibration on living organisms, discovered that the vibrations of a specific frequency could destroy bacteria, yet leave other living tissues unharmed. The frequencies that Rife produced were in harmony with human tissues, but disharmonious to bacteria and virus.

As early as the 1950s, Hulda Regehr Clark, PhD, N.D., has been studying biophysics, cell physiology, and the effects of electromagnetic vibrations on a broad spectrum of viruses, germs, and fungi. She spelled out in precise detail what frequency of electromagnetic vibration would destroy which organism. She backs this up with dozens of stories about her experiences in applying specific frequencies to specific organisms and the results she achieved.

According to Hulda, the main cause of illness is permitting our bodies to come into contact with food, personal care products, household cleaning products, or any environments that are not in harmony with the body to a greater of lesser degree. If the food, for example, happens to be in a pizza or a Big Mac, we may not experience any sudden reaction to what we've been exposed to, but that doesn't mean our bodies liked it. I buy most of my food at health food stores, and they are usually organically grown. Yet, I still had problems that took me to a Naturopathic allergist to discover exactly what I was exposed to that was not in harmony (an allergen) with my body.

Energy Sustains Life

I know groups of people on this planet that never eat food. They are sustained by the energy of the sun, elements in the air, or they absorb cosmic energy directly. Early in the 20th century Dr Hilton Hotima proved that our bodies never absorb solid or liquid foods. He proved that everything we put into our bodies always comes out. Our bodies do not need the solid food that we eat, but only the specific vibratory energy that the food imparts to our bodies. If an individual believes he or she cannot exist without food, then they have created their own reality and must eat food.

Molecular Imprinting

Molecular Imprinting is a way of adding a specific vibration to an existing molecule. The molecule can be any type of molecule - ranging from small molecules such as amino acids or vitamins to larger molecules like proteins. Small molecules such as water, acid or alkali are very easily imprinted. It is very easy, for example, to imprint a molecule of water with the life-giving vibrations of vitamins, minerals, enzymes, and amino acids giving the water nutritional benefits.

The Miracle-II products' successes are largely due to how they affect our bodies when applied. Primarily, these are three:

1. The manufacturing process is based on the very simple principle of polarity. Miracle-II products all vibrate at a polarity and frequency that is 100% in harmony with healthy human tissue. At the same time, their vibrations are disharmonious with any chemicals, organisms, or tissues that might be harmful to healthy human tissues. Harmful vibrations will be neutralized by Miracle-II.

2. Miracle-II has a very high pH (well above neutral 7.0) and, as we've discussed earlier, germs, virus, harmful bacteria, fungus, and parasites cannot survive in an alkaline environment.

3. Miracle-II is molecularly imprinted with all the vitamins, all the minerals, all the enzymes and all the amino acids that are required to promote and sustain a healthy body.

CHAPTER NINETEEN

Dimensions of Life - Part II
Introduction

In the previous chapter we asked the question: What are the components of this world that affect our health? The components that we stated were matter, energy, space, and time. We then called these MEST for short. We also assumed that, in our own sphere of influence that includes our own bodies, each of us have power over all of these MEST elements. Within our own world we can make them what we want them to be.

We also asked: What are the forces in the world that have, in the past and in the present, hindered us from using this power that we have to change our world? One of the more important answers that comes to mind is "understanding."

The focus of this series will be to improve our understanding of our MEST world so that we may better deal with the problems of health, wealth, and wellbeing.

The Nature of Energy

Earlier, we decided that energy is vibratory in nature, and that vibrations can have several qualities: frequency, wavelength, amplitude, polarity, and harmony.

Frequency is the number of occurrences or pulses in a specified timeframe. Our heart, for example, can have an average frequency of 50 to 70 beats per minute. Other parts of our body vibrate at much higher frequencies.

Harmony refers to one vibration's relationship to another. If we get a headache, for example, we know that some vibration in our head is out-of-harmony with the rest of our body.

Polarity refers to whether an energy field is positive (vibrating in a clockwise direction) or negative (vibrating in a counterclockwise direction).

The Nature of Matter

In 1903, a young civil servant living in Bern, Switzerland, and working in a government patent office, had an intense interest in the nature of our universe. The young man's name was Albert Einstein. It was in 1905 that Albert Einstein published five papers that shook the foundations of traditional physics and altered the course of scientific endeavor for all time. Among these papers was his now famous theory of relativity which stated that all laws of nature are the same if frames of reference are moving uniformly relative to each other. Another paper formulated his revolutionary mass/energy equivalence $E=MC^2$. Still another treated the quantum nature of light and its effect on matter, called the photoelectric effect. A fourth examined the irregular motion of microscopic particles in solid matter. Lastly, he developed his theories on the dynamics of atomic particles which today we call Quantum Mechanics. Einstein dared to imagine a universe so different from traditional thinking of the time that even today many brilliant minds have difficulty accepting it. When Max Born, a prominent physicist in his own right, read Einstein's papers, he was deeply impressed. "We were all aware," he commented in retrospect, "that a genius of the first order has emerged."

The most important of these papers for our discussion here is Einstein's mass/energy equivalence formula $E=MC^2$.

The Physics of Matter

Mass, in the formula $E=MC^2$, is defined as "a measure of inertia" which is defined in terms of kilograms, or, if you're English, in terms of pounds. Matter, by virtue of its resistance to motion may be considered mass. By solving E=MC^2 for mass we have M=E/C^2, or Mass = (Vibratory energy)/ (The speed of light squared). This is a very simple proof that mass is really just another form of energy. Under this definition, all sense objects in our environment become just another form of energy. The food that we eat, the air that we breathe, and, of course, our own bodies, are only energy that has taken on various forms according to its wavelength and vibratory rate.

What's the point? The point is that everything we wrote earlier about the nature of energy, including vibration, amplitude, harmony and polarity, also applies to all those solid-appearing objects around us, including ourselves.

Why is this important to our health? Because through a deep belief we "know" that we aren't really a solid physical being but a powerful ball of energy. If we can really convince ourselves of this, we have developed a powerful force for changing our own environment and our own health. We, ourselves, and everything around us, are constantly changing. We are not the same person we were yesterday. We will not be the same person tomorrow that we are today. Are we the one's controlling the changes that occur in our lives on a day-to-day basis, or are we surrendering our power to other forces around us -- The Matrix? It has always been difficult for me to visualize a steel girder, or any other solid object, as being constructed of vibrant, vibrating atoms until I had the following experience -

> I lived in Alabama for about seven years. One evening I was driving north from Montgomery, Alabama on my way home from a late night class at Auburn University. I had just spent three hours in class after a full days work at Gunter Air Force Base. I was tired, and my judgment was poor. As I approached my left turnoff near Wetumpka, AL, suddenly two headlights appeared over the hill in front of me. They were approaching rapidly, but I felt I could still make the turn before it arrived at the intersection. Only after I began the turn did I realize my error. As I turned into the oncoming

lane, the oncoming car was on top of me. I heard tires squeal and braced myself for the inevitable impact, I saw the two headlights on my hood, but the collision never occurred.

Still shaking from the incident, I tried to reason how a serious accident had been avoided. My only conclusion was that my eyes must have deceived me when I saw those headlights on my hood. I was deeply puzzled by this experience and wondered how I could have possibly avoided the collision.

Some months later, Dan, a friend and fellow seeker, shared with me an experience he had recently. Dan was driving on a narrow country road winding around a mountain side. Mountains were on his left and a steep drop into a jagged canyon was on his right. He was carefully negotiating a left-hand curve when a truck suddenly appeared from behind the mountain. It was traveling too fast to make the turn and drifted into Dan's lane. With the steep drop on his right, Dan had no room to avoid a crash. No collision occurred. Like me, Dan was also puzzled about how he could have avoided a serious collision.

Unlike me, however, Dan knew what had happened. He had a dream a few nights after his experience. He was sitting in a classroom being taught by a Spiritual Master. Dan got bored with the subject of the lecture. Suddenly, he jumped out of his seat and walked right through the wall next to his seat. As he did so, he remembers hearing a sound something like a buzz saw. He walked back and forth through the wall several times. Each time he could hear that sound - bzzzz.

The Master stopped his lecture to watch Dan. When Dan finally returned to his seat the Master explained that the bzzzz sound heard when Dan passed through the wall, was the atoms of the wall and Dan's body rearranging themselves so that no collision would occur. This experience proved to my satisfaction that spaces do exist between the atoms of a seemingly solid object.

Years later I shared these experiences with a friend and she shared an experience that she had while traveling on a heavily traveled freeway. She was traveling North in the passing lane with a steel barrier on her left separating cars traveling South, when suddenly a car on her right drifted into her lane. She swerved to her left into the barrier, but no collision occurred, and she ended up on the other side of the barrier facing south.

Creating Your Own Destiny

Many of us have heard about, or experienced directly, the power of our minds and attitudes to affect our environment, including our health. Many, who have refused to accept a doctor's death sentence, have been able to heal themselves by their attitude and thought process. How did they do it? They did it by understanding the forces that mold their future and the process of creating their own destiny.

I haven't been under the care of a traditional physician for nearly 40 years. The only time I get near them is when I go for a periodic checkup I do spend a lot of time deciding what my body needs to feel good by reading and searching on the Internet. These are all important to my health, of course, but not the most important.

I'm convinced that the most important attribute to good health is attitude and belief. Many of us will recall Jesus' statement that faith can move mountains. I still believe this. Then why can't I do it? It's because my belief isn't strong enough so that I "know" absolutely that the mountain will move when I tell it to. Why don't I have this kind of knowing? It is because of my conditioning and what I've been taught by those who dwell in The Matrix. Traditional science discounts any forces they can't understand, like the forces of mind and Spirit.

Because of these beliefs, I "know" I am not this physical body that I see in the mirror every morning. I "know" those terrible thoughts that can pass through my mind are not me. I "know" that those painful anxieties I experience are not me. I do, "know," however, that I am an energy being, eternal, and indestructible. The laws of Physics tell me so: Energy can be neither created nor destroyed, but only transformed to a new state. This is the attitude, I believe, that has saved me from the ravages of major illness.

About three years ago, I attended a seminar in Columbia, Maryland. To this day, there's only one thing I am able to recall from that evening. In the middle of one of the talks the speaker made this statement: "The most important decision you can make at any instant of your life is: What to think next." This is a decision I must make hundreds of times in the course of a day. I now know that whatever I decide will form the basis for my eventual attitude and, ultimately, my destiny – my health, my wealth, and my wellbeing. If I think angry, hateful, or fearful thoughts, I will never achieve the kind of love and happiness that is really what most of us seek. Today, whenever such thoughts enter my mind, I reject them immediately and replace them with pleasant, loving ones. This is my key for creating my own destiny. I try to be aware of where my thoughts are every second of the day, because I know that my attitudes and beliefs are sure to follow.

CHAPTER TWENTY

Dimensions of Life - Part III

Two very important points were made in the last two chapters: Part I, everything in our world is made of the same stuff, and Part 2 we showed that through our thoughts we can create a better world for ourselves. In Part III we will discuss the third part of our MEST world: Space. Is it really a void in outer space?

Early Research
It was Ptolemy, the Greco-Egyptian mathematician and astronomer, who, in the second century A. D., was the first man to propose the nature of outer space. In ever-greater spheres surrounding the earth, Ptolemy visualized the elements of water, air, fire, and ether. Beyond the ether he envisioned even greater spheres of heavenly planes.

While the bulk of Ptolemy's theory has been disproved, his theory that all of space is filled with some non-descript substance called ether has been accepted as fact for many centuries. If light is, indeed, a wave or vibration, then it needs some substance like ether to travel through. Ether had never been proven scientifically.

Then in 1881, two American physicists, A. A. Michelson and E. W. Morley, decided to prove, for all time, the existence of ether. Unfortunately, science mandates certain physical procedures must be followed before a proof can be accepted. Until man's instruments are sensitive enough to measure extremely high vibrational energy, science will never be able to totally accept the fact of ether. Here again we encounter the disadvantage of rigidly separating the subjects of Physics, Metaphysics, and Religion. Let's examine the proven facts according to physical laws.

Physical Laws

You will remember earlier chapters that mentioned what is called in physics "The Right Hand Rule." The rule has to do with an electrical flow through a conductor, like the electrical wires in our houses. The "Right Hand Rule" states that if we would grasp one of the wires in our house with our right hand, while our thumb points in the direction of the electrical flow, then our fingers would point in the direction of the electromagnetic force that surrounds the wire that results from that electrical flow. Since we know that our earth has a magnetic field around it, we must also assume that it is a conductor of some dynamic flow of energy. What is this energy? Could it be that great enigma ether?

If you have seen the movie *Star Wars*, you may recall a scene where Luke Skywalker and Obi Wan Kenobi were streaming through hyperspace in the Millennium Falcon, the spacecraft of Han Solo. Obi Wan was teaching Luke about the "Ways of the Force." "It surrounds us, it penetrates us, it binds the galaxy together," Obi Wan instructed Luke. Here, George Lucas, the author of the earliest Star Wars Trilogy, is implying that this energy Obi Wan has called "The Force" is everywhere, and it flows through "Every Thing." In *Star Wars* it is treated as real energy. It seems to be just another word for Ether, Orgone, Prana, Chi, or even Spirit.

Science has already accepted the fact that "Space" is not empty. Many physicists believe that space holds a powerful, dynamic energy, and that it's the same energy that flows through all of life including you and me.

The Dimensions of Life's Energy

Today we seem to know enough laws to survive physically, but what about laws that govern the more subtle aspects of nature: mind, emotion, and Spirit. These are all a part of the Whole of Life. Why do we so often fall victim to the hazards of life: illness, poor human relationships, and lack of finances to meet our basic needs? Could it be our lack of understanding of the more subtle laws of nature that we are subject to?

Quite often the more subtle laws of nature are more easily understood when we relate them to laws in nature. One law that can help in this case is the law of magnetism which states that, "Like charges (or polarities) always repel and unlike charges (Polarities) attract one another." This law is really about polarity. You may recall from an earlier chapter that polarity is one of the qualities of a vibration. Polarity refers to whether a vibration is positive or negative.

It should be no surprise to most of us that our thoughts also have a polarity. If I have thoughts of anger toward another person most would probably agree that this thought has a negative polarity. Thoughts of breaking the Ten Commandments or committing one of the seven capital sins should create the same effect. On the other hand, if I have loving thoughts toward another person most would agree that this is a thought with positive polarity. Practicing the seven virtues or one of the nine Beatitudes should have the same effect.

The important point to make here is that thoughts are vibrational energy possessing a powerful potential to do great harm or tremendous good, both for the transmitter, the receiver, and anyone perceiving or hearing about the good works.

All of this mental activity takes place at the more subtle levels of reality that we might call the spiritual aspects of life. You may recall that an earlier chapter mentioned the devastating effect that our thoughts can have on our physical bodies. I quoted from a medical encyclopedia that listed the physical effects of anger, impatience, anxiety, depression, or any form of stress. The adrenals secrete up to 28 hormones affecting virtually every system in my body, depending on how long one is in these states. My heart begins to pump more blood. My lungs begin to pump more oxygen and fuel to my body tissues. Lung passages dilate. More sugar is released into the bloodstream. Systolic blood pressure is increased, while time for blood coagulation decreases. Stomach and intestines contract and immobilize. Possibly worst of all, the thymus gland withers. *(The Encyclopedia of Natural Health* by Joseph B. Marion). The Thymus gland is the controlling force for our immune system.

Creating Positive Polarity

The negative energy that we generate when we are "stressed out" can be caused only by our thoughts; therefore, if we wish to avoid these negative effects we've got to begin with our thoughts. If we find ourselves caught up in waves of negative polarity and want to change that negative polarity to positive, we do it by changing our thoughts. There is a psychological law stating that the mind of man cannot think of more than one thought at a time.

Whenever I catch myself thinking thoughts that have the potential to create within me the vibration of anger, fear, anxiety, depression, vanity, lust, or greed, I shift my attention to a more powerful positive vibration. I can think of a pleasurable trip that I took or of someone I love, but I know of no faster way of dissolving negativity than singing, aloud or silently, a word or words with a powerful vibration. My favorite word to sing is the word HU. I've found that no negativity can stand up against the vibration of HU. So I sing within myself silently HUUUuuuu until the negative vibrations are consumed in HU.

Over the years I've acquired the habit of meditating every morning for half an hour. I sit in a comfortable position, place my attention on my energy centers that lie behind and between the eyes, and I sing, silently or aloud, the word HU. This practice maintains such a powerful positive energy around me that I've stopped being fearful as in my former years. Then during the day I monitor my thoughts and dissolve any negative ones with the word HU.

Impressing the Ethers

Earlier we mentioned that if light is, indeed, a wave or vibration, then it needs some substance like ether to travel through. We also know that the same truth holds for our thoughts since we can project our thoughts to a friend or relative. It also might follow that everything that we think, everything that we feel, every thing that we do, and everything that we say, forms an impression, a totally unique vibration, in the ethers.

CHAPTER TWENTY-ONE

Dimensions of Life - Part IV

Possibly the most important idea to be learned from the past three chapters is that we need to view ourselves, the people and things around us as energy beings rather than as gross physical bodies. Physics as well as religion have shown us that we are all made of the same stuff, and that, no matter what you call it -- ether, Orgone, the "Force," Chi, Prana, ECK or the Holy Spirit – we are all apart of that same whole.

The Enigma of Time

The 4th and final part of this series, time, has always been an enigma to me, mainly because of what I've heard and read about it. Metaphysics and some spiritual teachings will insist that "time is an illusion." An illusion is an erroneous belief, concept, or condition where our minds, through some logical thought process, have arrived at an erroneous conclusion. This view has always been very difficult for me to accept for most of my life, but I'm beginning to reexamine it from a new viewpoint.

Physicists, on the other hand, have shown mathematically that time is just another form of energy. We will examine both of these viewpoints

Time as a Form of Energy

We may recall earlier that when we wrote about Einstein's famous $E=MC^2$ formula and his Theory of Relativity. We saw that both theories dealt with the idea of two important factors concerning us here: Space and Time.

Though it may not be obvious, the formula $E=MC^2$ means Energy is equal to Mass multiplied by the speed of light squared. Speed means that light has traveled over a specified distance in a specific amount of time, or distance divided by time (d/t). We now discover that energy is actually dependant on time and visa-versa. Mathematically we could actually solve this equation for time and discover that a period of time is dependant on mass (matter) and energy.

Time as an Illusion

Ever since I've entered this "Great Spiritual Adventure" called life, the words "rapid change" were reflected in many of the teachings. Change, of course, takes place over a period of time. I've often heard words like "the speeding up of growth" and "the acceleration of time." I understood very readily "the speeding up of my growth," and I've surely experienced the change. "The acceleration of time" was not so easily understood.

Through many lifetimes I have become so locked into meeting schedules that waiting in grocery lines, in government offices, at cashier windows, waiting to pay off this bill, be free of that mortgage, and to trade in my old buggy for a new car that I always seem to be killing time waiting for the next event to occur. Since I've never been a patient person, waiting for the next event has never been easy. Time is certainly not an illusion when I'm waiting for that lady in the checkout line to count all her coupons, and write out her check.

When I recall other times while I'm enjoying a good book, a good movie, spending hours with loved ones, or being creative with my writing, time shrinks to nothingness.

If time is an illusion then it must be something deep within my own sub-conscious. If I can expand it like this or shrink it like that, then I must have a degree of control over time, and, therefore, something that I can learn to conquer.

What Other Writers Say

Many writers have written about time. I'd like to quote a few of them here:

One of my favorite books on health and healing is *Vibrational Medicine* by Richard Gerber, M.D. Here's what he had to say about time: "There is a concept of time which has been referred to as the 'eternal now' (or spacious present) whereby past, present and future may actually exist simultaneously but in different vibrational time frames. It is possible that by shifting the frequency focus of one's consciousness one may be able to tune into specific time frames outside of the present. In actuality, by shifting one's frequency focus, one may be shifting his/her consciousness from the viewing perspective of the physical up to the astral, mental, causal and higher energetic levels which are all a part of our total energetic expression." If you want truly in-depth wisdom on health, read Dr. Gerber's book.

When Dr. Gerber writes "shifting the frequency focus" he is saying essentially the same thing my newsletters have been stating for years. We have placed great emphasis on the importance of thought energy vibration, and where we focus our attention at any given time. Our attention gives our thought-forms greater energy thus making them a stronger influence on our future.

Too many people have written about their experiences of past lives and experiencing future events for me to doubt Dr. Gerber's statement that "past, present and future may actually exist simultaneously."

One of the best books I've ever read on the nature of our universe is called *The Holographic Universe* by Michael Talbot. In Michael Talbot's book he shares fascinating stories on time. He writes about a Russian-born Pole, Stephan Ossowieccki, one of the most gifted clairvoyants who lived in the early 20th century. While fully awake he had a vision of a past life where he was in a courtyard of a palace when a young attractive woman appeared. As he looked at her he knew instantly that she was an Egyptian and daughter of a prince. He could also visualize her husband as a tall, slender man. Stephan also saw a sequence of visions on the woman's life as though sitting watching a movie of her life.

This is just one of many stories Michael Talbot shares in his book. He also shared his stories about the future. He wrote of the experiments by J. B. and Louisa Rhine on predicting events. They discovered that volunteers picked at random are able to name what cards would be picked randomly from a deck with a success rate much better than chance. I'm sure we have all heard stories of psychics who predict future events more accurately than probability could predict.

How is this possible?

In his book *The Flute of God*, Paul Twitchell included a chapter called the "Book of Laws." Paul describes seven laws that govern these worlds we live in. These are not necessarily physical laws as defined in physics. However, laws of physics are in reality a mere reflection of strict spiritual laws that manifest at a higher vibration. Law number six of the "Book of Laws" is called:

> The Law of Facsimiles which is an overlaying law of the Law of Attitudes... Now facsimiles deal with those pictures you took in [your] mind. These pictures have been with you since you came into this world. They will influence [you] in one way of another... These facsimiles are merely little units of energy which gather about the body, mind and soul. They keep the attention of the individual 'I' on them, especially if they are bothersome pictures... The facsimile can control the individual to an extent that he becomes aberrated... Of course the flows of energy which are recorded in facsimiles are dead flows. In order for them to have any power or life, a new flow of attention must be played over them by the individual. So you see that no matter what is wrong with the individual, he is the one that is keeping it that way. This comes in with cause and effect... The chief aspects of cause and effect are the positive and

the negative. When an individual is cause [for a good purpose] he is being positive; when he is [the] effect [of somebody else's harmful cause] he is being negative. The art of good picturization is the art of full beingness.

Anyone with the skill can view these pictures or experiences that Twitchell wrote about can and bring his or her past into full view, or even predict his or her future.

Jesus taught this same idea when he said, "we reap what we sow." Many of us may also recall Newton's third law of motion which is a reflection of this higher law of cause and effect: "For every action there is an equal and opposite reaction."

Nullifying Time

While wrestling with this idea of time, a book that I read many years ago popped into memory. It was Paul Twitchell's science fiction novel *The Talons of Time.* I simply had to pull it off my bookshelf and take a fresher look at this incredible adventure story. I remember being so enthralled with the story that I couldn't put it down till I'd completed it. As with many a good science fiction story, there is always a strain of truth or some revelation about the future. This novel is no exception.

This is a story of Peddar Zasqe and Sharir, "The Magician of Lo," and their encounter with the "Time Makers." Sharir spoke to Peddar of a diary and the secrets hidden within it. "What is it you are looking for in that diary?" asked Peddar. "If we would learn what *The Talons of Time* are then we could learn the whole secret of this strange phenomenon of nature (time)," replied Sharir. This was the beginning of Pedar's compelling journey, his encounter with the "Time Makers" and his quest for the diary that would reveal the secret of time.

During his adventure he meets the beautiful Laos who becomes his constant companion in his search for the diary. After many months, their search leads to the palace of Kal Niranjan, Lord of the Underworlds. While secretly scanning the dark corners of Kal's throne room, Laos spots a book. "Could it be the diary we are searching for? I'm afraid to look," said Loas nervously. "I'll look," said Peddar reaching for the small book. Excitedly he examined the fly leaf. Finally he said: "This is the diary. This is what we've been looking for, Loas. Do you know what this means? This is escape for us. We must find a place of safety where we can read this wonderful book."

They finally discover a secluded spot in the far end of the castle. Peddar takes a seat in the dust and bids Loas to keep watch while he reads the contents. Nervously he turns the leaf to the first page and begins to read:

...Each moving body possesses its own standard of time and its own system of space to which an observer will always be in relation... Experience reveals the strange fluctuation of our sense of time when we approach the same fact from different points of view. Time shortens during love affairs and increases during painful hours.

...The movement of time is largely within ourselves. This is one of the implants that the 'Time Makers' have put into the human race. They have made us believe that the quick or slow passage of time is something subjective...

...There is no fixed past, but everyone has his own fixed past and future. We are terrified by the size of the structure and times which our thoughts create.

...Each observer lives in his own time, but the universe as a whole knows no time history. It is the same yesterday, today and forever... The universe, though describable in space and time to an observer, is neither in space nor time. This is the key to time...

...In order to conquer these illusions we must be able to acquire new habits of thinking of the system as a whole. In that case, there will be no time to bind us, but we can live in eternal freedom.

Here is what we've been stressing in these chapters. Only our thoughts, attitudes, and beliefs create the world we live in. We can nullify time, and any other conditions we don't like about our life, by thinking only thoughts that create the health, wealth, environment, and state of well being in which we really want to live.

CHAPTER TWENTY -TWO

The Spiritual Laws of Life - Part I

The Energy Spectrum

In this next series of chapters I will share a few of my experiences working with energies both physical and subtle. By subtle I mean energies of a higher vibration that manifest as thought, emotion, subconscious impressions, and even spiritual impressions. All of these energies are required to promote true holistic healing. The energies that I'm referring to don't merely suppress symptoms as the general populations seem to prefer: rather, they treat the whole person both physical and subtle so that healing can be more permanent. In order to accomplish this, however, a change of viewpoint, a change of attitude, or even a change in beliefs, is often required.

None of this is possible without an understanding of the laws that govern the more subtle realms of mind and Spirit. Violation of these laws is the main reason that we get sick, suffer, and die. Therefore, those ancient barriers that our institutions have constructed between science, psychology, and religion must come down. Then and only then will we understand what laws we violated that made us sick, and what we must do to get well.

We all know what happens when we violate physical laws. The Law of Gravity, for example; If we jump out of an aircraft without a parachute, we know that, unless we can fly, gravity will likely destroy the physical body. As a thinking and intuitive spiritual being, I have discovered a completely new set of laws that govern the subtle parts of me. These are not necessarily the laws of religious institutions that grew out of the teachings of true Masters like Jesus, Abraham, Mohammed, Pythagoras, Zarathustra or Buddha, but these often are the teachings that these true Spiritual Masters actually taught.

The Law of Attention

One of the more important laws of life is The Law of Attention. This is where illness of the body and mind begin. It is our thoughts that we propel with emotional energy that create an aura of attraction and repulsion around us often attracting what we hate and fear and repelling what we love and enjoy.

Quite often the more subtle laws of nature are more easily understood when we relate them to laws in physics. When we place our attention on a specific idea, for example, we have actually created an impression on what physicists call the ethers and what religionists call Spirit. We should never forget that thoughts are things that have vibrating energy with the power to produce an effect on us, as well as, those around us. The nature of the effect depends on our own past experiences that produce our state of consciousness, so it is always up to us to determine the nature of the effect.

Let me illustrate. I do a lot of driving in rush-hour city traffic which is a real challenge for most of us. Often I find myself a block away from a traffic light that is green. I race to get through the light, but it turns red too soon. All of these images have made impressions on my state of consciousness. At this point I have two options:

If I follow the same decision path that I have followed most of my life, I will jam on my brakes in a fit of anger, but if I recall the fact that thoughts and emotions are vibrational energy possessing a powerful potential to cause serious harm, or tremendous good, to both mind and body, I may shift my "Attention" to a different, more pleasant thought. I might also recall what I read in the medical encyclopedia that tells me what I can expect to experience physically whenever I permit emotions like anger, impatience, anxiety, depression, or any form of emotional stress; The adrenals secrete up to 28 hormones effecting virtually every system in my body. Please reference to Chapter 20, under sub topic of *the Dimensions of Life's Energy* the last paragraph. (Paraphrased from *The Encyclopedia of Natural Health* by Joseph B. Marion). The Thymus gland controls our immune system that attempts to reject toxins plus germ and viral invaders of the body.

The negative energy that I generate when I am "stressed out" can be initiated only by my thoughts; therefore, if I wish to avoid these negative effects I've got to begin with my thoughts. If I find myself caught in the waves of a negative emotion and want to change that negative to positive, I do it by shifting my thoughts that bring in a positive vibration. There is a psychological law stating that the mind of man cannot think more than one thought at a time, so positive thoughts will crowd out the negative thoughts that I have placed my "Attention" on.

Whenever I catch myself thinking thoughts that have the potential to create within me the vibration of anger, fear, anxiety, depression, vanity, lust, or greed, I shift my attention to a more powerful positive vibration. I can think of a pleasurable trip that I took, or of someone I love deeply. I know of no faster or more effective way of dissolving negativity than singing, aloud or silently, a tune or a word or words with a powerful positive vibration. These often turn out to be the name of a spiritual figure of the past like Jesus, Amen, or Yahweh. I have sung Jesus with the Latin pronunciation: Yezuuuu. True masters are obliged under spiritual law to respond to anyone who calls. Jesus has promised to do this.

I've been thinking what could possibly be more powerful than the vibration of "God." More recently I've learned what the ancient Masters used to call God. We can find this word embedded in the English language; in words like human and humor. This ancient name for God is HU. The HU has had a much stronger effect than any mantra I've used in the past. I've found that no negativity can stand up against the vibration of

HU, so I sing aloud or within myself silently HUUUuuuu until the negative vibrations are consumed in HU vibration.

There have been times when doing my daily contemplative exercises that HU actually seemed too powerful for my needs. Therefore, I searched for a deeper understanding of the effects of sound vibration on the human consciousness.

The Power of Words

The ancient Chinese Master Lai Tsi had contemplated for fifteen years in various caves and retreats high above the Yellow River in north central China. In reply to a question raised about his life there, he answered:

> It is the [Holy Spirit] that envelops all bodies of man within itself. These bodies are composed of the five selves, which are under the control of soul, and the words spoken by man. The words are seals of the mind—results or, more correctly stations—of an infinite series of experiences which reach from an unimaginably distant past into the present, and which feel their way into an equally unimaginably distant future. They are the audible that clings to the inaudible, the forms and potentialities of soul, that which grows and unfolds into perfection.

> The essential nature of words is, therefore, neither exhausted by their present meaning, nor is their importance confined to their usefulness as transmitters of thoughts and ideas; but they express at the time, qualities that are not translatable into concepts. This is like a melody which, though it may be associated with a deep meaning, cannot be described by words or by any other medium of expression. It is that irrational quality which stirs up our deepest feelings, elevates our innermost being, and makes it vibrate with those with whom we are closely related in love and work.

The birth of language was the birth of humanity each word was the sound equivalent of an experience connected with an internal and external action. A tremendous creative effort was involved in this process which extended over a vast period of time, and due to this effort man was able to rise above animals and other forms of life.

All that is visible clings to the invisible, the audible to the inaudible, the tangible to the intangible, and the thinkable to the unthinkable. The seer, poet and singer, the spiritually creative, the psychically receptive and sensitive, and the saint—all know about the essentiality of form in word and sound, in the visible and tangible. They do not dislike what appears small and insignificant, because they can see the great in the small. Through them the word becomes flesh, and the sounds and signs of which it is formed become the vehicle of mysterious forces. "Through them the invisible takes on the nature of symbols, the tangible becomes a creative tool of the [Holy Spirit], and life becomes a deep stream flowing from eternity to eternity. (*The Shariyat -Ki- Sugmad, Book Two,* by Paul Twitchell, P. 182-83)

In order to maintain that high positive vibration in my state of consciousness and build up inner energies, I contemplate/meditate every morning for half an hour. This prepares me for any difficult challenges I may encounter during the day. I sit in a comfortable position, place my attention on the "Energy Center" that lies behind and between my eyes, and I sing, silently or aloud, the word HU. This practice maintains such a powerful positive energy around me that others can sense it. It also builds up an aura of protection around me. This practice makes it much easier for me to control both my thoughts and the emotional effects of the thoughts that I place my attention. Then during the day, if negative thoughts do pop into my mind I simply dissolve them by shifting my attention to a brief, silent HU sing.

There is an alternative to this approach. Many of the higher masters have suggested that another powerful source of spiritual energy is the Heart Center. If you want to experience the true, unconditional love of God for you, place your attention at your heart center during your contemplations or spiritual exercises. You will be glad you did.

The Law of Attention, if obeyed, has the power to change our lives. It manifests its power every second of the day that we are awake. We must be fully aware of the thoughts that pass through our minds every second of the day. They all have powerful potential, to either heal or make us sick. It's up to us.

One of my past teachers suggested an exercise for me many years ago. At intervals during my waking day, he advised, stop and ask yourself: what have I just been thinking in this instant of time. After doing this for one day, I discovered that the flow of my thoughts are interminable and that most of them were negative, each with a potential to cause serious damage if charged with emotion. My mind constantly jumped from one thought to another – often flowing haphazardly and out of control. I have often permitted my thoughts to drag me into the worst snake pits of emotion that you can imagine -- all because I didn't understand The Law of Attention.

The Physics of Attention

What happens when I place my attention on an *idea, a place, or a person*? Here is what physicists say will happen. Recent discoveries in physics revealed that the electron appears to have the ability to manifest as either a particle or a wave, photon or quantum of energy. This appears to be an attribute of all subatomic particles. They can all change from particles to waves and back to particles again. Physicists have chosen to call this phenomenon with a dual nature, quanta. We all know that this is the "stuff" that our universe, including ourselves, is structured.

A still more astounding discovery about quanta is that it appears to be a particle only when a human is observing it. Renowned Danish physicist, Niels Bohr proved that the atom's quanta becomes a particle only in the presence of an observer, otherwise it is an unmanifested wave or bundle of energy.

David Bohm, a University of London physicist and former protégé of Albert Einstein took the work of Niels Bohr further. The next step in David Bohm's research involved his experiments with organized masses of electrons called plasma, where he found that single electrons ceased their random behavior and began to conform to the group's behavior. Electrons in a group seemed to take on the identity of the group acting as a single entity, even to the extent that it took on the organic quality of reproducing itself. Bohm actually got the impression that it was alive, took on a personality of its own, and seemed to be interacting with the observer.

Bohm's work with plasma lead him to conclude that the true nature of matter is not individual electrons acting alone, but rather they are a part of an integrated system purposefully acting for a single objective. Bohm concluded that the way an observer interacts with any group of quantum, determines what the physical result will be.

Bohm was apparently able to bend masses of atoms to conform to his own thoughts. To me, this is very conclusive proof that thoughts have energy and, no matter what they are pointed at, my physical body, my family, my coworkers, or thoughtless drivers on the highways, atoms respond to your and my "Attention."

Now I begin to understand what Bohm has demonstrated here in light of our discussion on the Law of Attention. Bohm has placed his attention on a quantum or waves of energy and it immediately manifests as atomic particles. He was then able to bend them to any shape he wished. What happens when we place our attention on a thing, a place or a person? Following are some examples from my own personal experience on the beneficial effects of attention.

Back in the 1970s I was living in foot hills of the Smokey Mountains. One of my close friends was a married lady in her 40s. She came to me with a troubled mind because she sensed that her marriage was breaking up. She was worried that she had no skills to support herself if her worst fears were realized. She wanted to take a course in typing, but she didn't have a typewriter on which to practice. I told her she would be welcome to borrow mine which was the latest model. Her rapid response was: "Oh, no, I could never do that. I'd only break it for you." After some serious convincing, I was able to convince her that she wouldn't break it, and, if she did, it could always be repaired.

A week passed and I received a phone call from a very distraught lady. "I knew it would happen," she cried. "Now I've broken your typewriter for you." I assured her that it was no big problem and we could get it fixed with little difficulty.

Here is the Law of Attention in action that produced a negative result. Breaking my typewriter, charged with the energy of Fear, was so strongly energized her consciousness that she actually created her own reality.

There are also many positive applications of the Law of Attention. Following is an example of the positive aspects of the Law of Attention.

The Chicken Lady is a young, attractive single lady who worked as a dental technician. She loved her job, but also had ambitions that took her much further than the dentist's office.

One of her greatest desires was to appear as a guest on the Oprah Show. She also had a very unusual talent which is how she got her name. She was exceptionally good at imitating a chicken. She was so good that no one could ever distinguish between her imitation and sounds roaming in the barnyard. But that's not all. She could also imitate other sounds equally well: a cow, pig, parrot, all kinds of birds, a police siren, and many others.

Much of her attention was focused on this very idea of performing her talents on the Oprah show. Every day she would sit down and write an account of just how it would happen. After some months, she decided to send for tickets to the Oprah Show.

The day finally came and she found herself sitting in the live audience of the Oprah show. Near the end of the show Oprah asked if there was anyone in the audience who had a special talent they would like too demonstrate for the audience. The Chicken Lady immediately jumped up screaming and waving her hand. She was called on to the stage where she demonstrated her skills.

Years passed and the Chicken Lady was called back to the Oprah Show to demonstrate her skills again, and share with the audience her life since her first appearance. She shared with the audience how she felt she had created her earlier experience on Oprah's show, and that it happened exactly as she had written it.

She also shared how drastically her life had changed. "I have always wanted to be married," she said, "but I didn't want to marry just any man. So I thought about the kind of man I wanted, then sat down and wrote a description of him in detail every day. This man didn't have to be royalty or even wealthy, just living comfortably. He didn't even have to be handsome, just normal. He did have to be loving with a good sense of humor.

She was now married and her husband was in the audience. He was a handsome, wealthy banker with many more qualities than she had envisioned in her written descriptions.

She advised the audience, "if you have a dream, write it down in as much detail as you can imagine every day. It will charge your dream with a shot of reality that will bring your dream to life." The Chicken Lady is living proof that if we build detailed images of what we want in our lives, write them down, and never place our attention on what we don't want in our lives, we are sure to be amazed at how much we can influence change for the better.

The Law of Attitudes

Up until about 30 years ago, my attitude toward heath pretty closely followed the way the masses view health: If my body displayed certain symptoms, I would take an over-the-counter drug, or call my doctor for an appointment. I gave my doctor total responsibility for my health, and I gave my insurance company or government the responsibility of paying for it. When I finally realized that the people involved here are not always responsible, I began to weigh my alternatives. I decided that I must learn more about the workings of my own body.

After years of study I learned that my body has all of the abilities, the functions, and facilities to achieve optimum health. I've also learned that every cell in my body knows the function of every other cell in my body. It's encoded in the DNA. This implies that every cell has a state of consciousness or awareness of its environment. Every cell knows the job it must do to maintain the health of the total system. This is a medically known fact. Each cell in our body has a function whose life is dedicated to the health and preservation of the whole community of cells, in a similar way that a colony of bees cares for its queen.

Have you heard about the people who have healed themselves after being told that they have only three months to live? Why does one person survive the doctor's death sentence while others do not? Attitude and belief are the reasons.

What is belief? According to Webster, it's a "conviction or acceptance that certain things are true or real." This implies that you are rejecting things that are not true or half true, like your doctor telling you that you have three months to live.

What would happen if you absolutely refused to accept such a sentence, and you absolutely knew that your body would heal itself if given the chance? I know the answer to this question, because I've tested it and proven it for myself which is the only way I could know for sure.

What is attitude? It's "a manner of acting, feeling or thinking that shows one's belief or opinion." If I believe that my body can be healed of any affliction, then I will think and act in the same manner. No fear or doubt will ever enter my consciousness. Fear and doubt are the villains in this play. You get rid of them by giving yourself the right experiences and avoiding the wrong ones.

As I look back, fear has been the bane of my life. Several years ago, I had to ask myself this question: How many of the decisions I've made in my life are based on fear? What fear are those decisions based on? I decided to make a list. Death is one of the greatest fears, but there was also fear of pain, illness, criticism, and fear of being wrong -- the list is endless.

All through my early religious instruction in Parochial Schools, I heard the words: "I must have faith, because faith can move mountains." I would always think to myself, "I'd love to have that kind of faith. How can I get that?" The answer would usually be that "it's a gift - The Gift of Faith." Today I don't believe we get anything for nothing. The question is: How can we earn faith?

Many years ago while taking the oral examination for my Master's Degree, I stressed the importance of a proper attitude while communicating ideas. The head of the department asked me: How do you change your attitude if it's not proper for your message? Without even thinking, the answer came from deep within me: Your thoughts create your attitude. Where you place your attention on a minute to-minute basis determines your attitude. I'd been given the key to attaining the "gift of faith," but to actually achieve it we must become aware of what we are thinking every minute of the day.

All too often I find my mind wandering off on its own to places I'd rather not be. Unless I have my thoughts under control, I can never be truly free. The fear of illness, pain, disease, and death will always plague me for the rest of my life if.

Over the years I've wondered about my own true nature. I have these feelings called emotions, and I have these thoughts that cause emotions. But how are these three parts of myself linked together? After much study I learned that there are physical parts of me called the Endocrine or ductless glands, and there are emotional parts of me called Chakras -- sometimes called Spiritual Centers. Most traditional medical practitioners do not recognize the existence of the Spiritual Center, but most Naturopathic doctors rely on them in their practice. The Naturopath will recognize the existence of another part of us that has a profound impact on the health of our physical bodies. They also recognize that the more subtle part of us called the Spiritual Center, communicates the wishes of the inner self by impressing the physical part of us called the Endocrine or ductless glands which scientists have learned influence - or even control - every function in the body.

When considering attitude we must answer questions like: How can I banish fear from my life: Fear of illness, fear of pain, and even fear of death? How can I avoid emotions that cause illness, like anger, depression, anxiety, and fear? Why has emotion been called the most devastating component of poor health?

After over 25 years of research into my attitude and its effect on my health, I could come to only one conclusion. I must maintain a positive attitude toward, not only my body's ability to keep me healthy, but of all experiences in life. I often tend to get upset while attempting to solve the endless problems I encounter on a daily basis: earning a living, paying my bills, and dealing with personal relationships at home, at work, and in everyday transactions. All of these have the potential to call up destructive emotions like fear, anger, hate, depression, lust, greed, and vanity. I am convinced that it's my attitude toward the endless variety of experiences I have every day of my life that ultimately determines the state of my health.

What do I mean when I say: "my attitude?" According to Webster, an attitude is "a manner of acting, feeling, or thinking that shows one's disposition or opinion." The key words here are thinking and feeling, which implies emotion. These are key because they are inseparably linked in the sense that it is my thoughts that determine how I'm going to feel emotionally. But what is emotion? Again, Webster says that emotion is "any specific feeling, or any variety of complex reactions with both mental and physical manifestations, such as love, hate, fear, anger, etc."

Emotion and Health

Now the big question: What does my emotional state, such as anger or fear, have to do with whether I get sick or not? To answer this question, we have to enter the field of psychosomatic medicine. Webster again says psychosomatic medicine proposes that an illness is "a physical disorder of the body originating in, or aggravated by, the psychic or emotional process of the individual." So here we have the implication, that if I get angry or fearful I could, somehow, end up in the hospital. So the bigger question is: what is this "somehow." How does this happen, or what is this linkage that can occur between what I think or feel and my illness?

Here's an example. I'm driving on a city street and, there's a green traffic light ahead. Shortly before I get there it turns red. I know it's one of those long, two-minute lights, but I'm too late to make it through. As I sit there at the intersection I can first feel a fire in the pit of my stomach. Gradually, it spreads to every nerve in my body, and I become tense and fidgety. All of this began because I thought about sitting at a traffic light, and I felt the light was red much too long. I was acting just like Pavlov's dog that salivated when a bell rang before food was ever seen. Psychologists would call my reaction to this experience a conditioned response. These feelings I had are called impatience, a form of anger, and are caused by secretions from glands in my body called the adrenals.

Whenever I react with emotions like fear, anger or impatience, the adrenals secrete up to 28 hormones affecting virtually every system in my body, depending on how long I am in this state.

Refer to Chapter 20 and the subtopic of *The Dimensions of Life's Energy* the last paragraph. (*The Encyclopedia of Natural Health* by Joseph B. Marion) Every system in my body is preparing me for action, but, in most cases, I do nothing. Every system in my body is now out of balance and has the potential to cause serious damage and malfunction in the body. Usually it's the weakest part of my body that is most vulnerable.

The eventual result of repeated adrenal reaction can be stress, anxiety, tremors, shock and counter-shock, bleeding stomach ulcers, high blood pressure, heart disease, anemia, lack of energy, insomnia, headache, depression, morose, self-consciousness, unhappiness, inhibitions, slow reactions, lack of interest, schizophrenia, and/or manic-depressive psychosis. (*The Encyclopedia of Natural Health* by Joseph B. Marion)

This reaction of the adrenals can be caused by any number of experiences: strange noises in the house at night, walking down a dark, deserted street, or criticized by a coworker. This sudden injection of adrenal hormones can be traced back to my attitude toward the experience that caused the emotional response of anger or fear.

Endocrine System

Most of us are probably aware that the adrenal glands are a part of a more complex system in our bodies known as the endocrine system. According to *Mosby's Medical Dictionary*, an Endocrine gland is "a ductless gland that produces and secretes hormones into the blood or lymph nodes. The hormones exert powerful effects on specific target tissues throughout the body. The [major] Endocrine glands include the pituitary, the pineal, the hypothalamus, the thymus, the thyroid, the parathyroid, the

adrenal cortex, the medulla islets of Langerhaus, and gonads."
The Endocrine System extends from the top of our head to the
lower part of our torso. "The building and constructive power of
man comes through the endocrines and their hormones."

This is important. This credible medical dictionary states
that "The building and constructive power of [physical] man
comes through the endocrines and their hormones." This is
the system that is affected by our emotions. Here is the link
between our psychological self and our physical self. In the
examples of fear and anger above, the psychological part of us,
our thoughts and emotions, caused a response from a physical
part of us, the endocrine glands called the adrenals.

In another example, diabetes is a condition where the
pancreas (a lesser endocrine gland) fails to react sufficiently
to a sudden surge of glucose or sugar and doesn't secret
enough insulin to balance the effect of all that sugar. This
occurs whenever the victim overindulges in high carbohydrate
foods. Here is a case where our attitude toward certain kinds
of food has caused an imbalance in the total physical system.
Knowing what we have to do to avoid this, we will alter our way
of thinking and avoid too many carbohydrates. Changing our
attitude can have an effect on our physical well being.

In spite of the many links that can be established between
our attitudes, our thoughts, our emotions, and our physical
well being, traditional medicine often neglects building such a
link between these more subtle aspects of ourselves, and our
chronic and debilitating illnesses. Holistic practitioners have
no such fear. Doesn't it make more sense to treat the whole
person: physically, emotionally, mentally, and spiritually.

Most of my life, I've fallen victim to all of the emotions that
I've mentioned here and paid the consequences. I finally got
tired of it and decided that I didn't want to have those unpleasant
and destructive feelings whenever that red light stared me in
the face, when I walked down a dark, deserted street, or when
I heard a strange noise in the house.

Changing Attitudes

The solution is simple to state, but not always so simple to accomplish. I began by distracting myself from the physical experience I was having by forcing my mind to think about something else. Whenever I found myself in a situation where I could feel those old familiar emotions creeping in, I forced myself to think about something more pleasant. Sometimes I would think about walking along Miami Beach breathing in that fresh, ocean air and sunshine. Other times I would think about those whom I have loved or have loved me.

The biggest advantage we have in dealing with our mind is that it can only think one thought at a time. All other thoughts loose their strength and eventually dissolve into oblivion when we give our full attention to thoughts that make us happy. Nobody really wants to be angry, fearful, or depressed. We really don't have to be if we realize that happiness, or unhappiness, are only states of mind brought about by whatever thoughts we are thinking at the time. We have the power to change our state of consciousness in an instant by merely changing our thoughts.

When I recall my past, I can remember times when my thoughts would carry me into some of the deepest fits of depression before I ever realized what was happening. Sometimes it would take me months to extract myself from them. Finally, I realized how important it is to be aware of where my thoughts are every minute of the day.

Several years ago I attended a lecture on the fundamentals of maintaining an emotional balance every waking hour. I'll never forget the one thing that was said that changed my life. The lecturer said: "The most important decision you can make at any given instant in your day is in response to the question: 'What should I think about next.'" Your answer will determine whether your state of consciousness will be a happy one or a sad one.

This was all a matter of reprogramming my thought process and changing the makeup of my subconscious. Just like Pavlov conditioned his dog when the bell rang, I conditioned myself to think loving thoughts in my times of stress. The loving thoughts that I conditioned myself to think eventually brought my adrenal glands into balance.

I must admit it is not always easy to shift my attention to pleasant thoughts when in a heated discussion or deeply depressed over some traumatic experience. Two techniques I have found to be especially effective are singing or listening to music. Giving my full attention to a tune that I love or a musical note that strikes a cord within me can perform miracles.

I've often wondered why certain music has such a profound effect on my state of consciousness. I got so curious about it that I decided to conduct a study of the subject. I've learned that, depending on our psychological makeup, we respond to specific vibrational frequencies found in certain music. We tend to like frequencies that help us feel more balanced. They are usually frequencies that may correct some imbalance in our physical or psychological makeup.

I've also learned that singing the vowels in our alphabet have a particularly high vibration. This is especially true of the letter "U." This is the reason that many people who meditate use what they call a mantra. A mantra is a word that, when sung, has a specific vibration that has been proven scientifically to bring about a calmer emotional state. Whenever I find myself in an unpleasant emotional state, I always sing the word "HU." I usually sing it silently drawling the vowel "U" out in a long HUUUUU. It has never failed to bring about a happier, calmer state of consciousness.

CHAPTER TWENTY -THREE

The Spiritual Laws of Life - Part II
Introduction

In Part 1 of this series I shared a few of my experiences working with energies including the physical and the subtle energies of mind, emotion, and Spirit. I stressed how all of these energies are required to promote true holistic healing and that a change of viewpoint, a change of attitude, or even a change in beliefs is often required to eliminate old destructive ways of thinking.

I also mentioned that none of this is possible without an understanding of the laws that govern the more subtle realms of mind and Spirit, and that violation of these laws is the main reason that we get sick, suffer, and die. Therefore, I suggested that we dismantle those ancient barriers that our institutions have constructed between science and religion to give us a better understanding of what laws we violated that made us sick, and what we must do to get well.

The first and most important law that we discussed is the Law of Attention. Essentially, the Law of attention states that whatever we place our attention on or think about in the course of our waking day will become our reality in the future. This means that if we think about cancer in a fearful way, then that reality will materialize in our life.

As I looked back on my own life I shared with you a few of the times when I unconsciously created experiences that I didn't want in my life, all because I wasn't aware of the Law of Attention. Now the next law we will discuss follows as a direct result of what we place our attention on.

The Law of Correspondence

"This is one of the greatest principles ever given in the field of thought," wrote Paul Twitchell in his master work *The Flute of God.* He was commenting on an obscure spiritual law called the *Law of Correspondence.* This law is very simply stated as follows: "As above, so below." This law may be found in the *Cabala*, the mystical teaching of the ancient religion of Judea. According to Paul Twitchell, our experiences in this physical world (below) are merely reflections of realities that we have created in the more subtle mental/spiritual realms (above). The symbol of Judaism itself reflects this profound teaching. It consists of two triangles, one that points upward superimposed on one that points downward to form the Star of Israel.

"As above, so below," is the second Hermetic Principle of which there are seven. These may be found in the *Kybalion*, a part of the *Cabala.* This book contains the writings of Hermes Trismegistus who lived in Egypt in the days of Abraham (of Biblical fame). Hermes, sometimes called "The Great," "The Master of Masters and scribe of the gods," is believed to be a teacher of the Old Testament's Abraham."As above, so below" contains the secret to understanding the Laws of Creativity, or how to create a better life for ourselves..

The Law of Correspondence might be considered the enforcer of the Law of Attention. To illustrate, let me share one of my own personal experiences with this law. When I got my first job after college I didn't have much money. Nearly every week my poor old car was in the garage for repairs. It was becoming a serious problem, since I needed my car to get to work. I had this in my "attention" often throughout the day. I literally caused my car to break down because that thought (above), charged with the devastating emotion of fear (above), was in my thoughts much too often. My attention on this problem set the Law of Correspondence into motion actually bringing my thoughts (above) into physical reality (below).

I've also discovered an even more important result of the Law of Correspondence. It also controls my ability to bring a change for the better into my life. As I give more and more of my mental energy (above) to the current realities in my life, like my car breaking down, not being able to pay my bills, or loosing my job, what do you suppose is going to happen at the less subtle levels of reality (below)? I am locking myself into my current realities whether I like them or not.

Through my attention I have created my current state of consciousness, how happy I am, what kind of a job I have, what kind of friends are attracted to me, and how healthy I am physically, mentally and spiritually. Here is an example of one poor soul whose attention has created an extremely sad state of consciousness for himself.

Misery & the Law of Attention
Some wonderful, sad person wrote this without disclosing his/her identity.

> I am alone and lonely. I want a companion. Other people have companions, why don't I? I have so much to give and want a person to share it with. I look around and see happy couples and wonder why I am deprived of this. I sometimes feel almost as though I am being punished! I just want to be loved.

> I hate my job. It doesn't give me any opportunity to develop my talents. I have much to give but no outlet for it. I don't know what to do. These people don't have any idea what I can do and couldn't care less. I want to be fulfilled but it won't happen here. I am so frustrated.

> My family treats me like an alien. They don't understand me; I can't count on them. They don't have any idea how I feel and they don't care. I try to get along but it is almost impossible to communicate with these people.

I have a hard time coping in the city. The traffic, the crowds, the smog, the prices (and it's not safe to live here). I do my best to get through it but I really live for the weekend when I can get away, or at least hide at home.

I am sick and tired of feeling sick and tired all the time. Enough is enough. This flu has lingered long enough and I'm fed up with not feeling good.

If I had money (REAL money) all my problems would be solved. I'm tired of struggling, of not having enough for a short trip or a new car or a few decent new clothes. Other people have these things and nice homes, and jewelry, etc., and I don't have. I haven't had the opportunity to get the money I know I could make if I just had the chance. Rich people I know of aren't any smarter than I am and don't work any harder than I would.

(from: http://www.is1.org/misery.html)

My heart goes out to this person, yet as I look back on my own life, I can identify with every feeling and emotion that this poor, unfortunate person was experiencing. I got pretty tired of those terrible feelings of helplessness and despair. It was wonderful to discover that I have the power to change all of that.

The Law of Attraction and Repulsion

Science has universally accepted that we all have an aura – an electromagnetic energy field surrounding us. A husband and wife team proved this many years ago. In 1939 the Armenian electrician Semyon Davidovich Kirlian (1900-1980) lived in the North-Caucasian town of Krasnodar. In 1963, Semjon and Valentine Kirlian, took out a patent on a technology that they called Bio-Electrography, later to be known as Kirlian photography. With a special camera they built, they were able to take photographs of very subtle energy fields. They took pictures of all sorts of objects, both organic and inorganic. They proved that we all have a magnetic field around us. This field, sometimes called an aura, has many colors. These auras are as unique to every individual as a fingerprint. Many scientists now believe that our aura is a reflection of the state of our physical, mental, emotional, and spiritual health.

During their experiments, the Kirlians once photographed a man with a missing hand (below) and found that his hand still existed at a more subtle level of reality (above), because the outline of the hand was defined by its aura. He also photographed a torn leaf he had pulled from a tree (below). The aura of the leaf defined a whole leaf (above).

Over the years, Kirlian photography has been refined and improved considerably to the point that it can be used in a way that is similar to traditional photography. Many alternative health and New Age expositions will feature a Kirlian photographer who will take pictures of an attendee's aura and explain what it means for that individual.

Science has also shown us that this dynamic electromagnetic energy swirling about us has an attraction and repulsion quality about it. We also know that the north pole of one magnet will attract the south pole of another magnet and repel the north pole of that magnet. These same principles may be applied to the electromagnetic energy of our own aura. Based upon the thoughts and emotional energies we have created, which make up our state of consciousness, we have built into our aura multiple attraction and repulsion energies. In a large part, we have created these energies by our strong opinions, our attitudes, our beliefs, our likes, and our dislikes accumulated over many lifetimes.

Many of my problems of the past had to do with relationships or lack of them; the relationships that I have with my family, my coworkers, my friends, and even with strangers I meet along the way. Everything I see around me in my life, I have attracted to myself because of the magnetic aura I have created around me. There have been times when the relationships that I have attracted to myself unconsciously were not to my liking. Much of the time it was not the fault of any other person, but rather my own attention and attitude that created the attraction or the repulsive energy surrounding me.

Here is one example. Through most of the 70s I was working for the Air Force in Montgomery, Alabama. I loved the work, the location and the southern people. I was attracted to Montgomery because of the harmony between my own electromagnetic energy and the energy created by the souls dwelling in that area.

But I have also learned that the magnetic energy of my aura also would draw to me difficult and unpleasant challenges needed to bring me to my next stage of spiritual development.

For most of my years in the South, I attracted wonderful relationships, interesting job tasks, and enjoyable social contacts. As we all know, the Law of Cycles and Vibrations do shift and reversals do occur. It is the nature of these lower worlds.

The end of the good times came when the government, my employer at the time, decided to downsize. They began what has come to be known as a RIF (Reduction In Force). Since I had seniority at this stage of my career, I did not fear loss my job, however, during that two year period, I was bumped from one unpleasant job to another until I ended up in the job all computer scientists love to hate -- a position managing old and "bug prone" computer software. The worst part of this shift was that I had been shoved into a position that several employees in the branch hoped to be promoted into. They resented me from the start and were determined not to cooperate with any of my efforts to succeed. Human relationships at this point in my life were at their lowest ebb.

I wanted out as soon as possible. For two years, I sent out hundreds of resumes' and applications all over the world. I became more desperate with each passing day. Few happy thoughts passed through my mind during those years, and, the saddest part is, I knew, at that point, about the Laws of Attention and Correspondence. But misery has a way of crowding out all wisdom and logic when we place our attention on current states of misery. As the saying goes, "when you're up to your neck in alligators, it's hard to remember that you should have drained the swamp years ago."

Through many cycles of trial and error, I have learned that I do have the power to lengthen or to shorten cycles through the Law of Attention. When I finally did remember the Law of Attention, I decided to stop struggling against my situation and find ways to enjoy the job and its relationship problems. I began to apply the Law of Attention by immediately rejecting any negative thought about my situation and replacing it with the powerful vibration of the HU song.

In less that a month the Law of Correspondence began to bring my new thoughts (above) into physical reality (below). An almost immediate reversal was apparent. My immediate manager, who was on a sabbatical, returned within the period of about three months. I had been hearing for years how tough this guy was, so I braced myself for the worst. He set up a meeting with each employee in his division. When my turn came, I told him all the details of the difficult situation I had been placed in, how I had been applying for other positions, and would probably accept my first offer. He listened attentively. Once I had finished, he reflected silently for a minute, and when he finally spoke, he hit a perfect strike right at my heart. "I don't want to loose you," he said, "so if you don't like this job the way it is, I give you total freedom to make this position whatever you would like it to be.

I was speechless. Considering what I had heard about this man, his offer was a total unexpected delight. I credit the Law of correspondence for changes that came into my life. However, I did have to initiate the thought patterns regarding the job and its relationships according to the Law of Attention. I also credit the energy field that I had created with the power to reach out and bring new and more exciting circumstances into my life.

CHAPTER TWENTY-FOUR

Spiritual Laws of Life - Part III

The first and most important laws that we discussed are the Laws of Attention & Correspondence. Essentially, the Law of attention states that whatever we place our attention on or think about in the course of our waking day will become our reality in the future. This means that if we think about cancer in a fearful way, then that reality will materialize in our life. The Law of Correspondence causes the manifestation of the forms that we have created with our thoughts.

The Power of Attention

As I look back on the experiences of my early years of searching, I can now see that spiritual law was in full force. Much of my early attention was on the relationships which I felt were causing my dilemma, and were powerfully charged with anger and anxiety. It was only after I removed those thoughts, that caused those emotions, from my attention that my situation did a complete reversal.

After my experience in Montgomery, Alabama, I received two job offers, one from NAS (The National Security Agency), and the other from SSA (The Social Security Administration). Even though it was less salary, I decided to accept the latter - a civilian agency that tends not to treat employees like they were in the military. Before I accepted the job at SSA, the interviewer did promise that I would be able to return to my original salary, probably within a year.

I loved the job and the people I worked with, and things went smoothly for the first year and a half. There was something in the back of my mind that relentlessly pushed its way into full view: still no salary increase. This became more and more a concern for me as I increasingly placed my attention on my current condition. I mentioned it to my supervisor as I was charged with ever-increasing angry energy. My relationship with him grew more strained.

This state of mind continued for another six months making me more miserable with each passing day. This state had totally overwhelmed what I knew in my heart about the Laws of Attention and Correspondence, but when they finally broke through to my conscious attention, I looked first at my relationship with my supervisor and how it had deteriorated over the past two years. I looked at his qualities as a human being and found them to have a very agreeable personality. He had a good sense of humor, always did the best for employees under him, and seldom bothered me about assignment completion dates. There was only one reason for any bad feelings between us: my attitude created by my own thoughts and emotions.

I took immediate action to correct this attitude. I first accepted totally my current state in the organization, salary and all. Whenever the salary thought came into my attention, I knew it was just another vibration that could be dissolved in another vibration: the HU song.

Before the next six months had passed, I received a salary increase, and to this day, I have a very enjoyable relationship with my former supervisor.

After these two experiences, I was convinced that I created my own environments by my thoughts and attitudes. With the experience in Montgomery, Alabama, I was placed in a very negative environment to begin with, and, through my attention, I became the effect of the vibrations in that environment. In the second example at SSA, I was the sole creator of that environment at the subtle mental level.

I've also discovered that I can also become the effect of subtle environments that others have created. Here is an example where subtle vibrations created by others affected my physical health as well as my mother's.

My hometown is Lancaster, Pennsylvania where my mother and only sister still reside. In 1995 I was still working at SSA in Baltimore and visited Lancaster as often as I could. Mother was in her 90s at the time and my sister felt it would be better if mother moved closer to her so better care could be given. We shopped around and found the ideal house just a few blocks from my sister. It was a small, well built stone house needing little or no maintenance.

The day of the move arrived. I drove up from Baltimore to help mother settle in, and I slept in the new house with mother overnight. In the morning we both woke up in a deathly ill state. I barely had the strength to climb out of bed. We were both in excellent health when we went to bed, so I had no clue as to why we should feel so bad. Then I recalled mother mentioning that the previous elderly owners were both suffering from a serious debilitating illness. It suddenly dawned on me that their house had been impregnated with the vibrations of that disease. I knew instantly what must be done. The vibrations in the house must be neutralized.

Mother and I sat down comfortably in the living room and began a contemplative exercise. We sang the HU song and imagined the vibration of that song filling every fiber of the house and surrounding area. We continued that for about twenty minutes. When we had concluded the exercise, mother and I could feel the difference, and that the illness we felt in the morning had mostly dissipated.

> Disease, as you know, is a disharmony resulting from the influence of an imaged picture. Music could return the balance if necessary, but one would have to reach the basic cause in order to erase the image.

Even certain localities and cities have their own wave lengths (vibrations) established by the souls living there. To live in surroundings where the wave lengths are compatible with your own makes for congenial surroundings, but to have to work in those where the vibrations are not at all in harmony will lead you to nothing but unhappiness. Hence, one will harmonize his surroundings with his own wave lengths, either adjusting himself or leaving. Unless this is done the individual will descend into misery.

This leads to a still greater truth; that the world itself vibrates on a certain wave length, and is, in fact, magnetic. No one will deny that the earth has magnetic poles called the North and the South poles. We also know that, owing to the composition of the strata of the earth's crust, different parts of the earth's surface are more magnetic that others, and throw out different wave lengths. It can easily be understood why one place suits one person more than another...
(*The Flute of God* by Paul Twitchell)

The Law of Vibration

Everything in our universe radiates energy, right down to the atom and beyond, and all radiated energy is vibratory in nature. Basically, this means that the energy varies in a regular periodic way.

Please keep in mind while reading this discourse that the performance of the atoms in our bodies is what affects our health. What happens to these atoms when we get sick will become clear as this series of articles proceeds.

Atomic scientists have already shown decades ago that when you can break up the atom into its smallest components, you end up with only energy. Atomic particles that appeared to be solid, when split apart, are really only energy.

When we visualize an electron, for example, we think of a tiny electrically charged sphere, but scientists have shown that it actually has no dimensions at all. What we could visualize is an electromagnetic energy field of varying strength and polarity that surrounds the nucleus of the atom instead of electrons. To place this phenomenon in human terms, the electromagnetic energy field of the atom could very well be called the aura of the atom.

The energy of the atom is perpetual. Every atom in our bodies seems to have unlimited supplies of energy. How is this possible? Such a concept would seem to violate every acceptable law of physics. What I am going to propose in the following paragraphs may seem like a giant leap over the beliefs of many. The following ideas do seem logical to me based on my research and the research of many broadminded scientists, as well as, churchmen.

The Energy Source

Physicist David Bohm, a University of London physicist and protégé' of Albert Einstein, implied in his masterwork, *Holomovement,* that a long list of the laws of physics appear to be a mere reflection of spiritual and psychological laws. Bohm astounded the physicist community with the pronouncement that everything in the universe is a part of a gigantic, ever evolving space-time continuum.

Bohm further concluded that dividing our world into animate and inanimate, organic and inorganic also makes no sense. Matter that we consider dead or inorganic still has energy, only in a different form. This idea has already been accepted under the "Conservation of energy" law which states that "energy can be neither created nor destroyed but merely transformed into another form."

Bohm has also shown that every cubic centimeter of empty space possesses the energy of the whole, even in a vacuum. What we finally conclude is that our world is constructed from a mass of powerful, intelligent entities that we are calling atoms, and that these entities have varying frequencies and polarities (positive or negative).

When I first read about Bohm's pronouncement that every cubic centimeter in our universe possesses the energy of the whole a past memory flashed across my mind. I recalled memorizing passages as a child in the early elementary grades. They were questions and answers from the Catechism of Christian Doctrine (Kincade's Baltimore Series of Catechisms - No.2). I picked the book off of the shelf and read: "Who is God? God is the creator of heaven and earth and all things. Where is God? God is everywhere. What is man? Man is a creature composed of body and Soul, and made in the image and likeness of God. Is this likeness in the body or in the Soul? This likeness is chiefly in the Soul."

Can we see the parallel between "God is everywhere" and Bohm's pronouncement that every centimeter has the power of the whole. Most deeply religious people believe that I know believe that "God is Omnipotent, Omniscient, and Omnipresent." In all good conscience, would it make any sense to say that God is everywhere except in the physical world?

If an all-wise, all-powerful God is everywhere, then Bohm's implication that "every atom possesses the energy of the whole, seems to be in perfect harmony with this Christian Doctrine and the beliefs of many other religions. This could also mean that every atom in our bodies is a part of God possessing the wisdom and the power of God.

It is perfectly understandable that many will find such a belief difficult to accept. One thing we do know, however, is that every cell in our body has energy and intelligence. Each cell in our body knows its own function as well as the function of every other cell in the body. Such intelligence is built into the DNA of every cell. The medical profession knows it, otherwise how could the body function so well for so many years considering the abuse that we and our health specialists shower upon it. It is not necessary that anyone believe these outrageous proposals in order to understand why we get sick and how to get well.

If I have all this power and wisdom dwelling in my own body, why do I get sick? If there is so much power and wisdom in every centimeter of the universe, why do we have polluted air, water, and food? Why don't we have a perfect world? – all good questions to be addressed in subsequent chapters.

CHAPTER TWENTY-FIVE

The Spiritual Laws of Life - Part IV

Let us accept what science has demonstrated. 1. The basic structural unit of our body is the atom. 2. Each atom is endowed with dynamic energy and intelligence.

The sciences conveniently represent vibration in the graphic form using the sine curve as seen in the figure below. Each sine wave shows two of the components of vibratory radiation: wavelength, and amplitude (strength). A third component, frequency is represented by the number of cycles that occur in one period of time (seconds, hours, days, years). We will deal with cycles-per-second in this study

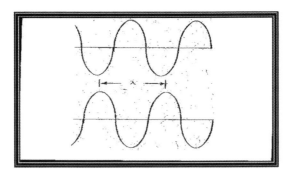

Measuring Frequency

Frequencies are measured in cycles, vibrations or pulses per second -- often called Hertz. The Hertz is usually the term used when computer scientists want to measure the time it takes for one computer instruction cycle. Everything in nature vibrates and, therefore, has a frequency. Audible Sound for example vibrates the air at 15 to 200,000 Hertz. Visible light has a frequency of $3x10^9$ to $3x10^7$ Hertz. X-rays have a frequency of $3x10^{15}$ to $3x10^9$ Hertz.

According to scientist Dr. Hulda Clark, the average frequency of a human body can range between 1,562,000 and 9,457,000 Hertz, insects between 1,000,000 and 1,500,000 Hertz and viruses, bacteria and parasites between 290,000 and 470,000 Hertz. She has catalogued hundreds of our bodily invaders. She has also discovered how to destroy them by exposing them to specific electrical frequencies and polarities that are intolerable to the organisms but do not have adverse effects on human cells. Drugs and herbal formulas with the proper frequencies and polarities have also been designed to destroy these organisms, but often with destructive side effects.

Polarity is the Key

In layman's terms polarity simply means opposite, as in light and dark, good and bad, right and wrong. In physics, polarity is the quality of having opposite magnetic poles as in north and south, positive and negative. In earlier newsletters I have written about the "Right hand Rule" that physicists use to define the polarity of an energy field. Whenever you have a flow of electricity (electrons or energy) through a medium (e.g., an electrical wire, your body or mine, or any atom in the universe) you will always have a field of electromagnetic energy surrounding it.

The reverse of this rule is also true. Whenever you find an energy field around anything, it is certain that a dynamic energy is passing through it. Therefore, when we experience an affect such as pain from anything that we ingest or put on our skin, we know that it is not the "thing" that causes the affect, but the energy field surrounding it. For example, my dentist tells me that it's not the mercury in my fillings that is harmful to my body; it's the energy that is surrounding it. The polarity of this energy, or any energy that is destructive to the human form, is considered negative energy.

Dr. Hulda Clark calls beneficial energy, "North Pole Energy," and destructive energy "South Pole Energy." Scientist and author, Ethyl Starbard, calls beneficial energy, Clockwise Energy and destructive energy "Counterclockwise Energy" because of the rotation of the energy field. The North Pole energy of our bodies enters the top of our head at the Crown Chakra and, according to the Right Hand Rule, creates energy swirling about the body in a clockwise direction.

Energy in the Body

Physical energy operations in the human body include: 1. the flow of blood through our circulatory system, 2. the flow of electrical impulses through the nervous system, and 3. the flow of cellular waste products through the lymph system. A blockage in any one of these systems can cause serious health problems and even death.

MDs use blood thinners or surgery to remove blockages from the veins. I use Miracle II Neutralizer.

MDs never diagnose blockages in the flow of electrical signals through the nervous system. Acupuncturists, massage therapists or chiropractors can use needles, pressure, or crystals to remove blockages from the nervous system.

MDs never diagnose blockages in the lymph system unless cancer is detected. Clearing blockages in the lymph system is entirely up to you and me – exercise. Walking, aerobics, or rebounding on a mini-trampoline are all good for pumping toxins from our lymph system.

All of these flows generate an energy field that surrounds the flow according to the right hand rule. If the force of our field (aura) is clockwise, then, according to the "Right Hand Rule," our energy is entering our bodies at the top of our head and flowing downward. Therefore, our polarity is considered positive. If the force of our energy field is counterclockwise, then the originating energy is entering the body near the base of the spine and our polarity is considered negative.

Everything in our universe has either positive or negative polarity. Let's say that the top sine curve in the above figure is considered positive and the bottom sine curve is considered negative. These curves have opposite polarities because when the one curve is curving up the other is curving down. If we were to add these two curves together mathematically the one would cancel the other and the result would be neutral energy.

Every system in our bodies is designed to achieve neutral polarity. Ingestion of carbohydrates, like grains, candy, or legumes causes a sugar imbalance that must be neutralized by insulin from the pancreas. Ingestion of acid-forming foods like grains, meat, or fish etc. must be balanced by either ridding the body of acid forming molecules through the kidneys or lungs, or neutralizing them by introducing alkaline-forming molecules (raw fruits, vegetables or Miracle II Neutralizer).

This neutrality must also be maintained in our more subtle aspects such as mental, emotional, and spiritual. This means we must strive to maintain our balance in these three areas no matter how many crises occur in our lives. The key to accomplishing this rests with The Law of Attention and The Law of Attitude.

The Law of Attitude states that whatever we believe in our hearts becomes true for us. If we believe the doctor when he/she tells us we have three months to live, then that will become our reality.

However, we can refuse to accept that pronouncement as our reality, and, according to The Law of Attention, remove that destructive thought whenever it enters the mind. We can create the reality that we desire by realizing, as physicist, David Bohm discovered that every cell in our body has the power and intelligence to overcome any malady.

Survival

As I look back on my life I begin to wonder what life is all about. Survival of the physical body is surely a major part of my daily activities. I have a job so that I can provide food, shelter, transportation, and pleasure for my body. This would appear to be the only goal in my life. As Jerry Seinfeld once commented about our body, "If it was a used car, we wouldn't buy it." We are stuck with it, and one goal should be to make it feel as good as possible so we can focus on more important goals.

The series of articles *Activating Healing Energies* is about our higher goals. When we are constantly dealing with the health of the physical body, we are consistently distracted from our real goal. So we are forced to deal with physical health issues first, and food is an important part of physical survival.

The Cells of our Body

I recently attended a seminar by Dr. Robert Morse, an internationally recognized authority in detoxifying the body. The three things that he said that impressed me the most are as follows: 1. "There are no incurable diseases," 2. "The cells of our body cannot long survive in an acid environment caused by the typical American diet (meat, potatoes and grains," and 3. Medical Doctors cannot heal, Naturopathic Doctors cannot heal, Homeopathic Doctors cannot heal, Acupuncturists cannot heal, and Detoxification Specialists cannot heal. The cells of your body are the only true healers. All these practitioners might do is to create a favorable energy environment so that each cell can do the job that its mission calls for: survival of the total being.

Every cell in our body is powerful, intelligent, and knows the function of every other cell in the body. Once we create the proper environment, all the cells of the body will work together as a single intelligent unit.

Have you ever observed a colony of ants or a hive of bees? Each individual in those communities know their job as well as the mission of the entire community as a whole: survival of the community. This is precisely the mission of every cell in our body. They will work tirelessly toward the survival of the entire organism. You and I are the only ones that can stop them. We hinder them by what we put into and onto our bodies, and, most importantly, by the mental/emotional energy that we have created with our thoughts.

What Do We Put into Our Body?

The general rule that we humans follow as we plod through life is: "Seek pleasure and avoid pain." With a little experience as an adult, however, we soon discover that this rule will often get us into trouble. I know a few of my friends would love to subsist on a diet of Big Macs, pizza and cokes. They give pleasure, yes, but they always result in what we don't want, pain.

When I first met Dr. Morse back in the 1980s, he was advising all of his cancer and aides patients to "Eat Raw Food." If they followed his advice their bodies healed naturally without radiation, chemo, surgery, or drugs. In his recent seminar he repeatedly emphasized the point that dead (cooked) foods are devoid of energy, and whatever the body cannot benefit from, it must expend energy to reject.

Once I became curious about why this is true, I stumbled onto a Web Site with the section entitled:

Raw Fresh Produce vs. Cooked Food (http://www.living-foodss.com/articles/rawfreshproduce.html)

What does cooking do to Nutrients in Our Food?

When food is cooked above 117 degrees F for three minutes or longer, the following deleterious changes begin, and progressively cause increased nutritional damage as higher temperatures are applied over prolonged periods of time: 1. Proteins coagulate and high temperatures denature protein molecular structure, leading to deficiency of some essential amino acids; 2. Carbohydrates caramelize ("Caramelized Carbohydrates" are said to be carcinogenic); 3. Fats - overly heated fats generate numerous carcinogens including acrolein, nitrosamines, hydrocarbons, and benzopyrene (one of the most potent cancer-causing agents known); 4. Natural fibers break down, cellulose is completely changed from its natural condition. It looses its ability to sweep the alimentary canal clean; 5. Vitamins & Minerals - 30% to 50% of vitamins and minerals are destroyed; 6. Enzymes - 100% of enzymes are damaged and loose their effectiveness as catalysts for essential cellular functions. The body's enzyme potential is depleted which drains energy needed to maintain and repair tissue and organ systems, thereby shortening the life span; 7. Pesticides found in most foods are restructured into even more toxic compounds; 8. Valuable Oxygen is lost; 9. Destructive Free Radicals are produced; 10. Pathogens - cooked food pathogens enervate the immune system; 11. Nucleic Acids and Chlorophyll - heat degenerates nucleic acids and chlorophyll; 12. Inorganic Minerals - cooking causes inorganic mineral elements to enter the blood and circulate through the system, which settle in the arteries and veins, causing arteries to lose their pliability. The body prematurely ages as this inorganic matter is also deposited in various joints or accumulates within internal organs, including the heart valves. As temperature rises, each of these damaging events reduces the availability of individual nutrients. Modern food processing, that usually requires high temperatures, not only strips away natural anti-cancer agents, but searing heat forms potent cancer-producing chemicals in the process. Alien food substances are created that the body cannot metabolize.

It may have been sufficient to say that cooking raw foods changes their polarity from positive to negative and their energy from clockwise to counterclockwise. This is in direct opposition to promoting the health of the body, thus causing injury to cells rather than nourishing them. Raw, living foods still have their vital LIFE FORCE in them, dead, cooked foods have none.

Mental/Emotional Energy

Earlier we mentioned that we hinder our cells from performing their assigned functions not only by what we put into and onto our body, but also by the mental/emotional energy that we have created with our thoughts.

If we are prepared to accept the fact that the cells of our body are powerful and intelligent beings as physicist David Bohm has stated, and what many holistic healers believe, then we must also believe that those same cells will be affected if we charge our thoughts with emotional energy such as *Fear or Anxiety*.

Take for example the person who believes their MD after he/she told them that they have cancer and will be dead in two weeks. This is a pronouncement that would strike fear into the hearts of most. The heart center is the spiritual power behind the thymus gland - the immune system of the body that would be responsible for keeping the cancer in check. Fear places a blockage at the heart center thus blocking energy flow to the thymus gland. Few, if any, T-cells are being sent out to attack the cancer. The thought/emotional energy of this patient has hindered the thymus cells from performing their assigned tasks just as effectively as the acid condition in the body, mentioned earlier. The death sentence will surely manifest, unless they make use of the Law of Attention to eliminate any thought of cancer and the fear that accompanies it.

CHAPTER TWENTY-SIX

Spiritual Laws of Life - Part V

The Law of Love

The Law of Love does state that this is the only way and the key by which the heavens may be opened and the truth and wisdom won and brought to light and service within the lower realms.

> All that exists does so because of love. Love of Sugmad (God) and between all souls is the fire that fuels the universe and the glue that keeps it together and continuing on its way and evoking and unfolding as all does cycle and continue to move and carry on. Love, though it is greatly misunderstood and maligned for other purposes and meanings, is the only thing that can bring salvation, and is the greatest power of all if used in the proper way. And so those who abide the Law of Love will always look for a way to express and utilize this frequency to bring the light of God and Its wisdom to all their endeavors and actions within this plane below.

> It is a simple case of the law that what you hold in your consciousness and give energy to in the

form of emotion and feeling does polarize your energetic field and draws to you that which you do fear most.

And the power of love and of the heart, and the wisdom and truth that is found there, is the greatest threat of all to those who seek by power and fear to maintain what they have achieved.

And fear is one of the key elements by which the heart is kept closed and the intuition and love and power from above from being heard.

But surrender truly is the key to surpassing the fear that grips the heart and is generated by the mind, and through surrender and vigilance and discipline and trust will the heart be truly opened and the goal be attained and realized. (*The Way of Truth Eternal, I,* By Michael Owens)

Imagine if the person who was given the death sentence by their doctor was a person who had no fear of illness or even death. Suppose they were a person filled with love and that love poured through their heart center like the whitewaters of the Salmon River in Idaho. Their thymus gland would be energized to generate enough t-cells to overcome virtually any outside invasion, be it germs, bacteria, virus, or pollution.

Miracle II Neutralizer is like a help mate of the thymus gland by neutralizing negative energy in the body.

Fear Blocks Love

Many years ago a survey was conducted to determine what kinds of fears are present in the general populations. Participants were asked to pick their greatest fears from a list, choosing their greatest fears first. Among the items on the list were: fear of death, fear of illness, fear of pain, fear of being criticized, fear of speaking in front of a group, and others. Interestingly, "fear of speaking before a group was most frequently listed above all the others, including fear of dying.

Over the centuries we have impregnated our consciousness with all kinds of fears. It has been said that fear is one of the major factors that prevent people from doing or saying what is really in their heart.

The one story that always touches me deeply is a real life experience about a young man who worked at a paper mill in a remote community near the U.S. Canadian border. One weekend he was driving down a deserted stretch of highway that led to the city where he bought his supplies for the week. One sunny morning he saw a number of cars parked along the road which was usually deserted. A group of people were gathered near the edge of the woods. He decided to stop his car to see what was going on.

After working his way through the crowd, he saw a big black bear sitting on its hind legs with its big front paws high in the air.

Right away, the young man could see the problem. The bear had thorns it its paws, so he hurried back to his car, returned with a pair of pliers and pulled the thorns from the bears paws. When he had finished, the bear ran off into the woods, and the crowd went about their business.

The man continued on his way, did his shopping in the city, and started home about 3 hours later. When he reached the spot where he had helped the bear, he again saw cars parked along the road and a group of people on the edge of the woods. Wondering what was going on now, he, again, parked his car and worked his way through the crowd. The same black bear was there looking at the faces in the crowd. Once he spotted the face of the young man in the crowd, he ran a short way into the woods, returned with two little baskets of blueberries, and carried them to the young man.

I'm sure there is another story just as interesting about a berry-picker who was frightened by a black bear. As difficult as this may be to believe, I've learned that nothing is impossible for the power of Spirit working through an open vehicle like the young man's. He loved life so much that fear of the bear never even entered his awareness.

When I first read this story, the only thing I could think of was: How can I achieve such a great unconditional love? The answer I received went something like this: If you want love to grow, remove fear from your consciousness. And "how do I do that?" I asked. The only thing that came to me was to place my attention at the heart center during my spiritual exercises. I was always taught to focus my attention on the spiritual eye that lies behind and between the eyes. Ignoring my old teaching, I began to place my attention at the heart canter during my exercises. I continued this practice for about a month, and, miraculously, many of my fears began to dissolve. One of my greatest fears, speaking before a group, almost disappeared completely.

As I continued this practice, other fears no longer plagued me: my fear of pain, my fear of illness, and my fear of death. With all of these fears gone, wonderful waves of love that I had never experienced before began to pour through my heart center.

These wonderful experiences eventually left me. How I know one of the barriers to that beautiful love experience: fear. Whenever fear returns, I merely place my attention at my heart center, and sing HU inwardly.

CHAPTER TWENTY-SEVEN

The Spiritual Laws of Life - Part VI

Review

Thus far in this series of articles we have addressed the following Laws of Life. Briefly, they are as follows:

The Law of Attention states that any thought, when charged with sufficient emotional energy, will become a reality for the thinker of that thought.

The Law of Correspondence, *As above, so below,* means that what we see around us in the physical world is a mere reflection of what has already occurred at the more subtle levels of reality: emotional, causal, mental, and subconscious..

The Law of Polarity is the law of the opposites where light is opposite to dark, sound is opposite to silence, and love is opposite to hate.

The Law of Balance states that every phenomenon in these worlds is the result of combining of two forces, positive and negative, plus the third force that is the balancing of the two called neutral. An acid/alkaline balance, for example would result in a neutral 7.0 pH.

Law of Vibration states that nothing rests; everything moves; everything vibrates.

Law of Conservation of Energy states that energy can be neither created nor destroyed but merely transformed into another form.

The Law of Love speaks to the relationships between love and fear, between love and the Heart Center, and between love and the Solar Plexus. We also discussed how we can achieve a love so powerful that all our fears will dissolve in the ocean of love that we have created. We have the power to create our own reality.

The Laws of Creativity

For many centuries man believed that the earth was flat and rested on the back of a giant turtle. Even today, small pockets of individuals gather together to confirm their belief in this theory. It's not so unusual when we consider the strong bonds that we humans form with traditional beliefs. It has been stated that the most powerful antigen known to man is a new idea. Under the Law of Assumption we "assume" that the realities created for us from our birth are true, and are the best available. Our institutions have created all forms of complex structures for us that affect every aspect of our lives, our finances, our work ethics, our family values, and what is good and what is evil. The recent movie has called these institutional structures *The Matrix* in which we have become entrapped.

Is all of what we've been lead to believe is true or even good for us? Evidence can be found throughout history that what we are being told is not necessarily true:

"Everything that can be invented has been invented." Charles H. Duell, Director of US Patent Office, 1899

"There is no reason anyone would want a computer in their home." Ken Olson, president of Digital Equipment Corp., 1977

"There is no likelihood man can ever tap the power of the atom." Robert Miliham, Nobel Prize in Physics, 1923

"Heavier than air flying machines are impossible." Lord Kelvin, President, Royal Society, 1895

"Video won't be able to hold on to any market it captures after the first six months. People will soon get tired of staring at a plywood box every night." Daryl F. Zanuck, 20th Century Fox, commenting on television in 1946

"This 'telephone' has too many shortcomings to be seriously considered as a means of communication. The device is inherently of no value to us." (Western Union internal memo, 1876).

Upon hearing Edison's announcement of a successful light bulb, Sir William Siemens, electrical engineer, asserted that:

"Such startling announcements as these should be deprecated as being unworthy of science and mischievous to its true progress."

"Louis Pasteur's theory of germs is ridiculous fiction." Pierre Pachet, Professor of Physiology, 1872

In reality, it takes a courageous individual with a vivid imagination to flaunt traditional beliefs in the quest for truth. Our history books are filled with stories of such men and women. Those who dared to be different, right or wrong have always stood above the crowd.

One such a man was Cladius Ptolemaeus more commonly referred to as Ptolemy, the Greco-Egyptian mathematician and astronomer, who, in the second century A. D., imagined his own view of the universe. He saw the earth as the center of a globular universe with the sun, moon, and stars revolving about it. Once accepted by the scientific community, the general public accepted his beliefs for centuries.

Then in 1530 a man with even greater vision proposed a different universe. He was the Polish astronomer, Nicholas Copernicus. Nicholas, while fulfilling his duties as canon of the cathedral at Frauenburg, East Prussia, completed his famous treatise on his view of the universe. This work, published in 1543 while its author lay on his deathbed, described a universe with its sun in the center and the earth as one of the planets which revolves about it.

It was in 1905 that Albert Einstein published five papers that shook the foundations of traditional physics, and altered the course of scientific endeavor for all time. One of his papers described his now famous theory of relativity which stated that all laws of nature are the same if frames of reference are moving uniformly relative to each other. Another paper formulated his revolutionary mass/energy equivalence $E=MC^2$). Still another treated the quantum nature of light and its effect on matter, called the photoelectric effect. A fourth examined the irregular motion of microscopic particles in solid matter (called the Brownian movement). Lastly he developed his theories on the dynamics of atomic particles, later called Quantum Mechanics. Einstein dared to imagine a universe so different from traditional thinking that even today many brilliant minds have difficulty accepting it.

Many believe that only by a total rejection of traditional beliefs was Einstein able to create such revolutionary concepts. Only by getting out of the rut of traditional thinking, wiping the slate clean, and starting anew can revolutionary growth is obtained. This way of thinking has become standard procedure for true creative thought, and, more importantly for us, the key to changing our lives for the better.

Many look at the swaying of the trees, the lay of the land, the howling of the winds or the unpredictability of the weather and see only chaos. It all seems to have no order to it. "God does not play dice with the Universe," insisted Einstein. As for Einstein, he saw perfect order.

Prominent men of science who have studied the creative process have arrived at the same conclusion. Thumbing through the Oxford Dictionary of English, one may stumble onto the term "lateral thinking." Lateral thinking is a way of thinking that would be considered illogical by traditional standards. The term was coined by Dr. Edward deBono, who has held faculty positions at Harvard, Oxford, Cambridge, and London. Dr. deBono believes that to think creatively we must first jar our minds out of the grooves that habit has formed, and chart brand new points of view. He has felt that only by blazing new trails of thought are individuals able to shatter current molds, solve life's problems, and mold a better life for themselves.

Early pioneers of flight felt that, in order to fly, wings had to flap like those of a bird. It took a man of vision to reject this image in favor of something as revolutionary as a propeller -- and still more revolutionary, a jet. Many designers of vehicles felt that wheels were essential to locomotion on the ground. It took a vivid imagination to invent the hovercraft -- a vehicle that rides on a cushion of air, or Magnetic Levitation (MagLev) that rides on a cushion of magnetic energy.

This pattern of thought has also been taught by great spiritual giants of the past. Jesus, in his parables about sewing a new patch on an old garment, and placing new wine in old wineskins, was also emphasizing the necessity of giving up the old in order to make room for the new.

In his letter to the Corinthians, Paul of Tarsus wrote, "When I was a child, I spoke as a child, I felt as a child, I thought as a child. Now that I have become a man, I have put away the things of a child. We see now through a mirror in an obscure manner, but then face to face. Now I know in part, but then I shall know even as I have been known."

Paul Twitchell, who has adapted the ancient teaching of Eckankar to the ways of modern man, has often taught that in order to be successful in a teaching that has broken free of tradition, we must forget everything we ever knew about philosophy and religion in the traditional sense.

The teachings of the masters have made clear the secret of what we must do to bring about beneficial changes in our own lives. Only by turning our backs on our traditional beliefs, ways of thinking or points of view are we able to break the molds that lock us into our current way of life. This process of change begins with our own beliefs, attitudes, and ways of thinking.

When the clouds darken the sky we say, "It's going to rain today." When we begin to cough and to sneeze we say, "I'm catching a cold." When we approach the age of 80 we say, "I'm in my final years. For the most part our beliefs and attitudes are based on what we have been taught, or what we have experienced in the past. We have been told that specific causes must produce these inevitable effects. Our senses tell us that these are all true. Are they, really? Perhaps it's true only because everybody believes them. Nearly every spiritual teaching in existence today stresses the invincible power of belief.

Einstein, Edison, and the Wright Brothers were all criticized severely for their beliefs. They had to be courageous enough to reject existing beliefs in order to blaze new trails in science. What do you suppose would happen if we rejected many of our own programmed beliefs behind us just like the scientific giants did? Could we also create a brand new future for ourselves merely by using our own innate creative abilities in harmony with the Laws of Creativity?

Too often we tend to feel that we are victims of life instead of its creators. Perhaps Einstein was wrong: "God does play dice with the universe." Maybe we are mere pawns in a giant chess game between God and the devil. However, we have each been given free will. We have the ability to make our own choices. This means that the life we are living today, the objects, the people around us, the experiences we have every day, were created by us through the choices we made every minute of the day. We are victims only because we have failed to break well-ingrained molds. We have failed to reprogram fixed thought patterns that are like a broken record -- repeating the same Pavlovian, stimulus-response program over and over again.

When we see those clouds in the sky we could say, "I can see the sun shining in my minds eye. Soon it will be a sunny day." When we begin to cough and to sneeze we imagine how good we will feel by the end of the day. When we reach retirement age we should say, "It's time to begin life anew."

Once we have established the mindset that all past conditioned beliefs no longer apply. We begin to create a new future for ourselves. Here are a few simple rules using the powerful Law of Assumption to create a new direction for our lives:

> 1. "Creating the image" - The first rule states that if we believe something strongly enough, and we can imagine it vividly enough in our minds eye, then reality will be molded around that image. This is the rule that has created our past. This is the rule that can build our future.

> 2. "The Law of Assumption" - We now apply a spiritual law, called the Law of Assumption, or "acting as if" our imagined reality has already materialized. Once we have created a detailed image of what we want to have in our life, we must now place ourselves in that environment. We feel the joy of it and the anticipation of immersing ourselves into it ever more fully. We think it mentally, and we feel the joy of it emotionally.

> We actually become a part of the images that we hold in our minds minute-by-minute. We aren't thinking about the problems of the past and the anxieties they caused, or what we would like to

happen in the future. We are already living in what we have created.

3. Action - We decide what physical activities we must perform in order to create, live in, and maintain this new reality. We are confident that all physical and mental forces will come into alignment with our own thoughts, feelings, and actions. We must be aware of those forces that will constantly want to drag us back to the old stuck-in-the-mud state of consciousness. Whenever those thoughts persist, we must shift our attention back to the new image we've created.

Here we have the keys to beneficial change. 1. Wipe the slate clean, 2. Create the image, 3. Live that reality mentally and emotionally, and 4. Take any physical action required to bring life to that reality. Think it, feel it, and act out that reality.

CHAPTER TWENTY-EIGHT

Mystery Schools – Part I

The Secret Teachings

Every religion or spiritual teaching has had what we might call their "secret teaching" that has been withheld from the general public. This was not necessarily for selfish reasons or because they wished to retard the spiritual progress of the masses, but rather because their attitudes or beliefs were too advanced for easy acceptance of the more advanced or esoteric teaching. Jesus also understood this need and reserved special teachings and benefits for his disciples and those who were diligent enough to glean Jesus' deeper teachings that are hidden deeply within his parables. "He (Jesus) will open his mouth in parables; He will reveal things hidden since the foundation of the world." (Isaiah).

Anyone who came to Jesus and asked the meaning of his parables, which the disciples did often before they were enlightened by the Holy Spirit, "He answered and said unto them, Because it is given unto you to know the mysteries of the kingdom of heaven, but to them it is not given... Therefore speak I to them in parables: because they seeing, see not; and hearing, they hear not, neither do they understand."

Jesus also stated it this way: "Give not that which is holy unto the dogs, neither cast ye your pearls before swine, lest they trample them under their feet, and turn again and rend you." Matthew|7:6.

The Purpose of the Mystery School

The objective of The Mystery School is to illuminate the individual consciousness by applying ancient teachings that are inscribed in the hearts of all people, and are reflected in the symbols that we see around us every day. In the Mystery School teaching, each person is on his or her sacred mission to become aware of, and be illuminated by, their true selves which is Soul. Members of the Mystery School are taught how to create a conscious affiliation with the spiritual realms, and to become fully aware of multi-dimensional resources. We live in a time when we can fulfill this mission now, rather than later. The choice is ours.

The Mystery School in History

One of the first known Mystery Schools was The Mystery School of Onnas. The ancient Greek city of Gadara was built on top of an even more ancient city called Joutthal in which the Mystery School of Onnas first started around 2350 BC., and endured for many centuries. It taught the spiritual mysteries of Egypt. The Essenic Mystery School of Mt Carmel was where Greeks like Pythagoras, Plato, Socrates and Aristotle received their advanced spiritual knowledge.

The Mystery School of Onnas held an envelop within time and space that was subtly removed from the rest of the world. When one entered the consciousness (or merkabah) of Onnas, one would feel a profound shift in ones awareness that allowed an access to deeper levels of the Spirit-Self than could be accomplished by being in the 'outer' world.

According to Onnas teachings, the Merkaba is the divine light vehicle used by the Masters to connect with and reach those in tune with the higher realms. The Mer-Ka-Ba is the vehicle of Light mentioned in the Bible by Ezekiel. "Mer" means Light. "Ka" means Spirit. "Ba" means Body.

The 'New World' knowledge represented the primary phase of spiritual evolution that the planetary consciousness experienced at that time. However, there was a small remnant of the Mystery School of Onnas which did continue past the time of 2345 B.C. (The mystery school continued its operations into the 3rd century B.C.).

The Essenic Mystery School taught astrology, numerology, and reincarnation, plus other subjects. The school was started at Mt. Carmel around 1386 B.C by a man called 'Japhael' who was believed to be from Scotland. In ancient times Mount Carmel was the centre of an ancient mystic tradition which established the seed of what became known as the Essene Brotherhood, and the communities that then existed in the Greek and Roman cultures.

Two thousand years ago, a brotherhood of holy men and women, living together in a community, carried within themselves all of the seeds of Christianity and future western civilization. This brotherhood--more or less persecuted and ostracized--would bring forth people who would change the face of the world and the course of history. Indeed, almost all of the principal founders of what would later be called Christianity were Essenes--St. Ann, Joseph and Mary, John the Baptist, Jesus, John the Evangelist, etc. They had knowledge of the hidden mysteries of nature and natural law unknown to other men. They considered themselves to be also a group of people at the center of all peoples--because everyone could become part of it, as soon as they had successfully passed the selective tests.

They felt that they had been entrusted with a mission, which would turn out to be the founding of Christianity and of western civilization. They were supported in this effort by highly evolved beings who directed the brotherhood. They were true saints, Masters of wisdom, hierophants of the ancient arts of mastery. The Living Spiritual Master of Jesus time was named Zadok.

Pythagorean Mystery School was founded by Pythagoras who traveled extensively. He had the benefit of the best possible education in his day. He had an insatiable thirst for knowledge which led Him to travel until the age of 56. During these years He studied under the sages of Egypt, the wise men of Phoenicia, Babylonia, Chaldea, Persia, and India.

Interestingly enough, Pythagoras lived at the same time Buddha was teaching His philosophy in India. While He was in Persia He studied the teachings of Zoroaster. It was from His stay among these foreigners that Pythagoras acquired the greater part of His wisdom.

On His return from His travels, Pythagoras established The Pythagorean Mystery School in Crotona where He taught the "Pythagorean Life". In this school, he taught the many things that he had learned and studied in His travels: from the Egyptians he learned the science of mathematics; from the Chaldeans he learned the science of astronomy; and from the Magi of Persia and the Brahmans of India e learned the science of living.

Pythagoras was both a founder of new sciences and a moral reformer. He was one of the first philosophers in the west to recommend a vegetarian diet. For breakfast Pythagoras would eat chiefly honey. For dinner He used bread made of millet, barley or herbs, raw and boiled. The new religion He taught was called "Biosophy". This is a word coming from the Greek roots *bios* meaning life, and *Sophia* meaning wisdom. Biosophy, hence means the wisdom or science of living.

Pythagoras made a sharp differentiation between learning, knowledge, and wisdom. Wisdom He saw, as being far superior to the first two. Learning is what we memorize and are taught by our parents, teachers and books. It is second hand information. Knowledge comes from what we know in our experience. Wisdom was the distilled essence of all that we have gained from life's experience. Pythagoras' main aim in life was the development of this wisdom of living.

Unlike the educational methods today, Pythagoras did not place each subject in a different pocket. He really only taught one subject that included: mathematics, music, physics, chemistry, biology, astronomy, religion, and the many related subjects. What link could he possibly find among such a broad and diverse array of subjects?

Pythagorean mathematics of nature stressed that all things consist of numbers, literally. In his *Harmony of the Spheres* those numbers took on the nature of cycles and vibrations. Pythagoras understood, perhaps better than anyone of his time or since, the effect of vibration on nature, on our health and on our state of consciousness. Mathematical systems that he established still hold up in today's modern world.

When I first encountered the Pythagorean Theorem I didn't fully understand the full significance of it: $a^2 + b^2 = c^2$. I had no idea how that could be applied in my day to day living. But more recently the name Pythagoras persistently keeps popping up in my research. I was reading a text that called his celebrated theorem "one of the most important discoveries in the history of mathematics." I was so impressed that I decided to dig more deeply into the man's life.

Pythagorean mathematics of nature stressed that all things consist of numbers, literally. In his *Harmony of the Spheres* those numbers took on the nature of cycles and vibrations. Pythagoras understood, perhaps better than anyone of his time or since, the effect of vibration on nature, on our health, on the human condition, and on our state of consciousness. Mathematical systems that he established still hold up in today's modern world.

Then suddenly it dawned on me what the practical application of the Pythagorean Theorem was. It defines the mathematical system commonly used to define cycles and vibrations: trigonometry. As we may recall, it's trigonometry that permits physicists to compute components of vibration using the sine and the cosine: frequencies (How fast does it vibrate?), wavelengths (How far does one vibration travel?) and amplitudes (How much power is behind the vibration?).

Unfortunately, the schools in which he taught these deep spiritual truths were not public schools. Students who applied for admission had to pass very strict tests. Many were turned away, and those who gained entrance were sworn to secrecy.

As mentioned before, the teachings of Pythagoras did not place each subject in a different pocket as our public schools do today. He really only taught one, all-inclusive subject that included: mathematics, music, physics, chemistry, biology, astronomy, religion, medicine, and related subjects.

The Numbers of Pythagoras

Pythagoras viewed numbers as a living thing, something which was not invented but discovered. He assigned to them a physical quantity like the motions of the heavens, the flow of energy through the body, or in the structure of the atom. He felt that numbers are divine and universal, and their reach went far beyond the physical dimensions into the sacred dimension of the mind and spirit.

Pythagoras called the number One, the Monad, the principle of Unity from which all things begin. Here again, we see the oneness of the "Everywhere God" discussed earlier.

The number two he called the Dyad or Duality. In the number two he foresaw the splitting of God's energy into good and bad, light and dark, male and female, agreement and conflict. This splitting of energies was both the beginning of strife, and the possibility of separateness among things and people, as everything no longer appears the same as oneness does.

He called the number three the Triad which forms a bridge, allowing the development of relationships between two extremes. Three allows for building bridges between two opposing views, compromise, harmony, and, eventually, love of all life. Each of these three concepts has deep spiritual implications for any spiritual seeker.

Unity of all Life

The Pythagoreans had four branches of Number: 1. Arithmetic consisted of solely Number, 2. Geometry was Number combined with space, 3. Music was Number in time, and 4. Astronomy was the mixture of Number, space, and time.

Hermetic Mystery Schools

Hermes Trismegistus established the Hermetic Mystery School. The foundation of Hermes teachings was the seven Hermetic Principles:

1. The Principle of Mentalism states that "The all is Mind; The universe is mental." A part of the Principle of Mentalism is Mental Transmutation which states that "Mind (as well as the elements of the earth) may be transmuted from state to state."

2. The Principle of Correspondence is "As above, so below; as below, so above." Everything created in this physical world has its origin in the heavens, or at a higher state of consciousness.

3. The Principle of Vibration is that "Nothing rests; everything moves; everything vibrates." It's the Pythagorean Theory of Numbers.

4. The Principle of Polarity is that "Everything is dual; everything has poles; everything has its pair of opposites." Thus we have light and dark, good and evil, right and wrong.

5. The Principle of Rhythm asserts that "Everything flows, out and in." This represents the balance of the two opposite polarities or neutrality.

6. The Principle of Cause and Effect states that "Every Cause has its effect." This is a manifestation of Newton's Second Law of Motion: For every action, there is an equal and opposite reaction. Or from Old Testament Law: An eye for an eye and a tooth for a tooth. Or from the New Testament: as you sow, so shall you reap.

7. The Principle of Gender states that "Gender is everything; everything has its Masculine and Feminine principles; Gender manifests in all planes."
http://www.eupsychia.com/myst/wksp/myst203desc.html

Knights Templar Mystery School

The <u>Knights Templar</u> have many references in <u>popular culture</u>, most of them quite inaccurate. The truth is that they were a Christian military order that existed from the 1100s to the 1300s, in order to provide warriors in the <u>Crusades</u>.

In modern works, the Templars are generally portrayed in one of two ways; as villains, or representatives of an evil secret society (e.g. <u>Mumbo Jumbo</u>, by Ishmael Reed), or as the keepers of long-lost relics such as the <u>Ark of the Covenant</u> from the <u>Old Testament</u>, or the <u>Holy Grail</u> (e.g. <u>Indiana Jones and the Last Crusade</u>).

Gnostic Mystery school

Jesus Christ was a Gnostic. Gnosticism is the path of directly experiencing the Divine as the path to salvation. Mysticism, Gnosticism, and the Jewish Kabbalah are all very similar. Their path to God is to look for God within ourselves. If we take the view that God is within everything, that nature and the universe is the very embodiment of God, then our own inner Self is the most accessible point for experiencing an all-pervading Supreme Reality. This Gnostic view is powerfully presented by Jesus in Luke 17:20-21: "And when he was demanded of the Pharisees, when the kingdom of God should come, he answered them and said, The kingdom of God cometh not with observation: Neither shall they say, Lo here! , lo there! for, behold, the kingdom of God <u>is within you</u>. *Luke 17:20-21, KJV*

Rosicrucians

A different class were the Rosicrucians (a secret society), who claimed to originate in 1407, but rose into notice in 1614 when their main text <u>Fama Fraternitatis</u> appeared and claimed to combine the possession of esoteric principles of religion with the mysteries of alchemy. Their positions are embodied in three anonymous treatises of 1614 mentioned in Richard and Giraud's, <u>Dictionnaire Universel des Sciences Ecclésiastiques</u>, Paris 1825, as well as in the <u>Confessio Fraternitatis</u> of 1615. Rosicrucians also claimed heritage from the <u>Knights Templar.</u>

The Illuminatti

The Illuminati is the name of many groups, modern and historical, real and fictitious, verified and alleged. Most commonly, however, The Illuminati refers specifically to the Bavarian Illuminati, perhaps the least secret of all secret societies in the world.. Most use refers to an alleged shadowy conspiratorial organization which controls world affairs behind the scenes, usually, a modern incarnation or continuation of the Bavarian Illuminati. Illuminati are sometimes used synonymously with New World Order.

Since Illuminati literally means 'enlightened ones' in Latin, it is natural that several unrelated historical groups have identified themselves as Illuminati. Often, this was due to claims of possessing gnostic texts or other arcane information not generally available. (References and Links: Wikipedia)

Freemasons

The essential qualification for admission into and continuing membership is a belief in a Supreme Being. Membership is open to men of any race or religion who can fulfill this essential qualification, and who are of good repute.

Freemasonry is not a religion, nor is it a substitute for religion. Its essential qualification opens it to men of many religions and it expects them to continue to follow their own faith. It does not allow religion to be discussed at its meeting.

Knights of Columbus

Mystery School sponsored by the Catholic Church, and has secret initiations up to 4.

Egyptian Mystery schools

For more than 3,000 years, the mystery schools of Egypt have epitomized the ultimate in secret wisdom and knowledge. As in ancient times, certain contemporary scholars and researchers insist that the great teachers who presided over the Egyptian mystery schools had to have come from some extraordinary place. Perhaps, it has been theorized, they were wise masters who survived the destruction of the lost continent of Atlantis, and made their way to the early civilization of Egypt where they helped elevate it to a greatness far in advance of other cultures of that era. Some have even suggested that the entity known as the god Osiris was an extraterrestrial astronaut from the Pleiades, who first visited Egypt in prehistoric times when it was composed of barbaric tribes. Because he came from an advanced extraterrestrial culture, say the proponents of this theory, he was considered a god and became the founder of the mystery schools and raised the primitive Egyptians' standard of living to a remarkable degree.

A Mystery School for Our Time

During times of rapid change and radical uncertainty, such as now, an inner process activates to link us to the wisdom of our ancestors, and opens the way to the God Worlds! The esoteric Mystery Schools are the preservers of this inner wisdom, an oral tradition transmitted afresh for every Age. The Ancient Mystery Traditions are the reliable "technicians of human consciousness" that restore the balance between our inner and outer realities, and lead us across the chasm of the unknown, guided by the perennial wisdom of those Masters who have trodden the path to inner wisdom.

A Mystery is a sacred event - like a death or rebirth - which creates a psychic shift and moves you to a new place in consciousness. Mystery Schools are made up of 'soul families' who come together to manifest a certain evolutionary function for the sake of humanity.

If there ever was a successor to the Pythagorean Mystery School, it would have to be The Way of Truth. (www. TheWayofTruth.org)

WEB SITE SOURCES

www.AbundantHope.net

www.agora-inc.com/reports/600SCTDF/
  W600DB98/home.cfm

www.aquatechnology.net/system_comparisons.
  html

www.**breatharian**.com

www.Dateline.MSNBC.COM

www.drclark.com

www.eupsychia.com/myst/wksp/myst203desc.html

www.fluorideACTION.net

www.Gods Herbs.com

www.hsibalitmore.com.

www.infinite-energy.com/iemagazine/   issue61/
  chargeclusters.html

www.inspiredliving.com/airpurifiers/ozone.html

www.is1.org/misery.html

www.living-foods.com/articles/rawfreshproduce.
  html

www.living-foods.com/articles/rawfreshproduce.
  html

www.mercola.com/

www.mercola.com/2000/jul/30/doctors_death.htm

www.Miracle-II.com

www.nrdc.org/water/drinking/bw/bwinx.asp

www.plasticbottles.com.au/products.html

www.saveourenvironment.org
www.scorecard.org/chemical-profiles/
http://thyroid.about.com/
www.timesonline.co.uk/article/0,,8123-978120,00.
    html
www.treedictionary.com/DICT2003/index.html
www.Waterwise.com
www.en.wikipedia.org/wiki/Lymph_node
www.TheWayofTruth.org

BIBLIOGRAPHY

Bohm, David, Holomovement, http://en.wikipedia.org/wiki/Holomovement

Clark, Hulda Regehr, The Cure for All Diseases, New Century Press, Chula Vista, Cal.,1995.

Clark, Hulda Regehr, The Cure for HIV and Aids, New Century Press, 1993.

Douglas, William Campbell II, M.D., Cumberland Blues, daily dose e-letter titled *"Fighting Back Against Flouride"* (10/31/03).

Dowling, Levi, The Aquarian Gospel of Jesus the Christ, Standard Publications, Inc, 2006.

Email: from AbundantHope.net by Candace, Christ Michael and General Radetsky, *Speak Strongly* January 5, 2008, 20:12.

Email alert: Health Sciences Institute.   *Fluoride time again, November 13, 2003*

European Parliament, *European Union Directive on Dietary Supplements,* Http://www.thefactsaboutfitness.com/news/eu.htm

"Exercise Makes You Smart: Study with old and young mice", USA Today, *September 21, 2005*

Future Technologies Newsletter, Author, Ed Leary,. email: futeck@tampabay.rr.com

Gerber, Richard, Vibrational Medicine, Bear & Company, 2001.

Greenleaf, Robert, The *Servant Leader*, 2003, Paulist Press, Mawah, N.J.

Guimond, Richard J., *Affects of Electronic Pollution*, Office of Radiation Program U.S. Environmental Protection Agency given to Subcommittee on Oversight and Investigations, U.S. House of Representatives, March 8,1990.

Hotema, Dr. Hilton, Man's Higher Consciousness, , *Health Research,* 1998.

Huggins, Hal A., It's all In Your Head, *Penquin Group, Inc., USA.,* 1993.

Indiana Jones and the Last Crusade *Director Steven Spielberg*, Paramount Pictures, 1989.

Jasmuheen, Living On Light,, *Konrad Halbig,1998.*

Kincade, Baltimore Series of Catechisms-No.2, Doubleday, Ny,Ny, 1995.

Marion,Joseph,B, Anti-AgingManual:The Encyclopedia of Natural Health,InformationPioneers Publishing,1993.

Mosby, Mosby's Medical Dictionary, *Health Sciences Division,* 2005.

NBC. Dateline, *The Power of Faith,* NBC, New York City, NY.

New Age Journal

New Testament, Oxford University Press, Ny,Ny, 2002.

Old Testament, Oxford University Press, NY,Ny, 2002.

Owens, Michael Edward, <u>The Way of Truth Eternal, Book 1</u>.*N.Y. BookSurge, LLC, 2005,*

Raum & Zeit, Space and Time, journal, bimonthly.

Reed, Ishmael, <u>Mumbo Jumbo</u>, Simon and Schuster, 1996.

Rew, Kate, <u>Time</u>, (UK Version), *Mind Over Matter,* January 27, 2004.

Richard and Giraud, <u>Dictionnaire universel des sciences ecclesiastiques</u>, Paris 1825.

Shames, Richard and Karilee, <u>Thyroid Power,</u> Harper Collins, 2001.

Soanes, Catherine and Angus Stevenson, editors. <u>Oxford Dictionary Of English</u>, Oxford University Press, Inc., 2004.

*Star Wars (movie),Lucas, George(Director), 20*th *Century Fox, 1977.*

Starfield, Barbara, Dr., *Journal of American Medical Association (JAMA)*: 284)(4):483-5, July 26, 2000.

Talbot, Michael, <u>The Holographic Universe</u>, Harper Collins,*1992.*

The Matrix (movie), Wachowski brothers(directors), Warner Brothers, *1999.*

The Passion of Christ (movie), Gibson.Mel(director), 20th Century Fox, 2004.

Thompson, Jenny, <u>Health Sciences Institute</u>. *"Bad to the Bone",* (4/29/03), and *"Don't fill 'er Up"* (2/13/03); web site at <u>www. hsibalitmore.com</u>.

Trowbridge, Tom, <u>The Hidden Meaning of Illness</u>, Association For Research and Enlightenment (A.R.E.) Press, *1996.*

Twitchell, Paul, The Talons of Time, *Eckankar Publisher, 1990.*

Twitchell, Paul, The Flute of God, *Eckankar Publisher,1989.*

Twitchell, Paul, The Shariyat-Ki-Sugmad, Book 2, *Eckankar Publisher,1998.*

Tucker, William J., Harmony of the Spheres, *Pythagoras.* 1950

Webster, David, *Dictionary*

Wikipedia: 2001 to present, free encyclopedia that anyone can edit.   Multilinqual, web-based, free content encyclopedia project

Wilder, The Cabala, Thornton Kissinger Publisher, 2004

INDEX

186
assumption, law of, 173, 178
astronomy, 78, 183, 185
atoms, 4, 5, 9, 10, 25, 28, 29, 33, 34, 45, 46, 79, 87, 88, 89–90, 91, 92, 93, 94, 95, 97, 109, 110, 115, 116, 136, 157–158, 159, 160, 161, 174, 185
ATP (adenosine triphosphate), 26
attention
    law of, 131, 132, 135, 136, 137–139, 147–148, 152, 163, 167, 172
    physics of, 135–136
    power of, 154–155
attention deficit disorder (ADD), 61
attitudes
    changes of, 1, 99–101, 102–103, 130, 145–146, 147
    as counterproductive, 107, 108
    as created by thoughts, 141
    a creator of emotions, 155
    defined, 140, 142
    effects on health of, 86, 98, 117, 141, 142, 144
    law of, 139–140
    power of, 117, 118, 129, 140
attraction, law of, 150–151
auras, 48, 90, 97, 131, 134, 150–151, 152, 158, 162
autoimmune disease, 70, 71, 73

B
bacteria, 8, 27, 38, 70, 96, 110, 112, 161, 169
balance, law of, 172
barium, 68
beliefs
    changes in, 1, 94, 130, 147, 177
    as counterproductive, 107, 108
    defined, 140

effects on health of, 117
    power of, 117, 118, 129, 140
benzophrene, 19, 165
BEV Water System, 17
bio-electrography, 150
biophysics, 45, 65, 110
Biosophy, 183
bladder cancer, reducing risk of, 12
blood and cardiovascular toxicants, 67, 68, 69, 70
body snatchers
    drugs and the FDA, 62–63
    endocrine system. See endocrine system
    heavy metals. See heavy metals
    parasites. See parasites
    pollution. See pollution
body workers, 61
Bohm, David, 29, 90, 93, 94, 136, 158, 163, 166, 192
Bohr, Niels, 93, 136
Born, Max, 114
boron, 23
bottled water, 16
breast cancer
    and deodorants as factor in cause of, 53, 68
    reducing risk of, 12
Breatharian Institute of America, 7
breatharianism, 6, 29
Brooks, Wiley, 7
Brownian movement, 175
Brujos Scientific Inc., 9
Buddha, 2, 131, 183

C
Cabala, 79–80, 148, 195
California Public Health Department, 38
Canada, chemicals used in large amounts in, 58

198

distillers, 17
dizziness, 69
DMPS, 74
DMSA, 74
DNA (deoxynucleic acid), 25, 26,
71, 72, 91, 139, 159
Douglass, William Campbell, 14,
16, 192
Dowling, Levi, 104, 192
drug companies, 62, 63
drugs, prescriptions for, 4, 62, 86
Duell, Charles H., 173
dyad (duality), 185

E
earth, magnetic field of, 46, 47,
120, 157
eating habits, 22. *See also* foods
eck, 29
ECK, 92, 124
Eckankar, 177
Edgar Cacye Book Catalogue, 57
Edison, Thomas A., 174, 177
EDTA (ethylene diamine tetra
ocetate) chelation therapy, 73, 74
education, concerns with traditional
form of, 76–78, 90, 99, 120, 147,
183
Egyptian Mystery Schools, 188–
189
Einstein, Albert, 29, 90, 114, 125,
136, 158, 175, 176, 177
electric radiation, 35
electromagnetic energy, 71, 75
electromagnetic environment,
32–48
electromagnetic fields (EMFs),
36–37, 150–151, 158, 161
electromagnetic low frequency
(ELF) radiation, 35–36
electromagnetic radiation (EMR),

36, 38, 41–44, 45–48
electromagnetic vibrations, 110
electronic pollution, 35–37, 94
electrons
Bohm's research on, 93–94, 136
as bundle of energy, 92
effect of cathode ray tube (CRT)
on, 34
and the Electron Gun, 32
as entropic in nature, 46
and kinetic energy, 88
as particle, 92, 135
as radiation, 33
visualization of, 89, 158
as wave, 135
electroradiation treatment
testimonies, 42–44
ELF (electromagnetic low
frequency) radiation, 35–36
elimination, in the body, 26
eloptic (electro-optical) energy, 49
EMFs (electromagnetic fields),
36–37, 150–151, 158, 161
emotional balance, 145
emotional energy, 21, 108, 109,
131, 151, 164, 166–167, 172
emotional health, aura as reflection
of state of, 151
emotional instability, 69
emotional self, 80
emotional stress, 132
emotions
as aspect of nature, 121, 141
as created by attitude, 155
defined, 142
destructive emotions, 100, 101,
132, 141, 142, 143, 145, 154
effects on health of, 100, 144
and the endocrine system, 144
as energies manifested, 1, 130,
131

201

Is Your Water Safe to Drink?
(Consumer Reports), 17
It's All in Your Head (Huggins), 70,
72

J

Japhael, 182
Jasmuheen, 7, 29, 193
Jesus, 2, 7, 29, 79, 80, 87, 103,
104, 117, 128, 131, 132, 176,
180, 182, 187
jogging, 30
John the Baptist, 182
John the Evangelist, 182
Johns Hopkins School of Hygiene
and Public Health, 83
Johnson, Milbank, 39
Joseph, 182
*Journal of the American Medical
Association* (*JAMA*), 62, 82, 83,
86, 194
Joutthal (city in ancient Greece),
181
Judaism, 80, 148, 187
juices, 22

K

Kabbalah, 187
Kaiser Permanente Medical Care
Plan, 37
Kelvin, Lord, 174
kidney toxicants, 68, 69, 70
*Kincade's Baltimore Series of
Catechisms*, 91, 159, 193
kinetic energy, 88, 92
Kirlian, Semyon Davidovich, 150
Kirlian, Valentine, 150
Kirlian photography, 150–151
Knights of Columbus, 188
Knights Templar Mystery School,
187

knowledge, Pythagoras on, 183
Kubzansky, Laura, 98
Kybalion, 80, 148

L

lab tests, concerns with, 63, 64, 73
lateral thinking, 176
law of assumption, 173, 178
law of attention, 131, 132, 135,
136, 137–139, 147–148, 152,
153, 154, 163
law of attitudes, 139–140, 163
law of attraction and repulsion,
150–151
law of balance, 172
law of conservation of energy, 2,
90, 158, 173
law of correspondence, 148–149,
152, 153, 154, 172
law of cycles and vibrations, 152
law of facsimiles, 127
law of gravity, 2, 130
law of love, 168–169, 173
law of magnetism, 121
law of polarity, 109–110, 172
law of repulsion and attraction,
150–151
law of vibration, 157–158, 173
law of vibrations and cycles, 152
laws, physical laws, 1, 2, 120, 127,
130
laws of creativity, 148, 173–179
laws of life, 172
laws of motion, 2, 186
laws of nature, 121, 131
lead, 59, 69
learning, Pythagoras on, 183
Lee, Dennis, 54
leukemia, 68
life
laws of, 172

mildew, 8
Miliham, Robert, 174
mind
    as aspect of nature, 121
    and dealing with change, 87
    power of, 117
minerals, 19, 20, 97, 165, 166
Miracle-II Deodorant, 53
Miracle-II Moisturizing Soap,
    52–53
Miracle-II Neutralizer, 21, 50–52,
    73, 75, 162, 163, 169
Miracle-II Non-Moisturizing Soap,
    53
Miracle-II products, 8, 10, 49–53,
    97, 111, 112
Miracle-II Skin Moisturizer, 53
miracles, of Jesus, 104
misery, 149–150, 152–153
Mohammed, 2, 131
molds, 8
molecular imprinting, 111–112
molecules
    acid-forming molecules, 163
    alkaline-forming molecules, 163
    binding molecules in fluoride, 14
    from bonding of atoms, 25, 33,
        79, 87, 88
    and frequency, 46
    metal molecules, 68
    and molecular imprinting, 111
    types of, in body, 25
monad (unity), 185
Morley, E. W., 119
Morse, Robert, 6, 19, 20, 30, 164,
    165
Mosby's Medical Dictionary, 143,
    193
Mother Theresa, 104
motion, laws of, 2, 186
motion of microscopic particles in

solid matter, 114, 175
multiple sclerosis, 42
Mumbo Jumbo (Reed), 187, 194
music
    according to Pythagoras, 185
    effects of listening to, 146
My Journey Through the Matrix
    (Leary), 107
Mystery School of Onnas, 181, 182
mystery schools, 181–189
mysticism, 187

N
National Council on Patient
    Information and Education, 62, 86
National Resources Defense
    Council, 13
nature, laws of, 121, 131
Natures Sunshine, 74
naturopathic doctors, 20, 61, 141,
    164
NBC Dateline, 103, 193
Neo (fictional character), 107, 108,
    109
nervous system, 162
nervousness, 69
neurotoxicants, 68, 69, 70
New Age Journal, 32, 193
New Testament, 186, 193
New World Order, 188
Newton's Second Law of Motion,
    186
Newton's Third Law of Motion, 2
nickel, 59, 68, 70
nitrogen
    in body, 25, 27, 28
    in farming, 23
nitrosamines, 19, 165
"North Pole Energy," 162
nucleic acids, 20, 25, 26, 166
numbers, according to Pythagoras,

Trowbridge, Tom, 79, 194
true self, as represented by "above," 81
Tsi, Lai, 133
Tulley, Charles, 40
Twain, Mark, 76
Twitchell, Paul, 79–80, 109, 127, 128, 134, 148, 157, 177, 195

U
ulcers, 143
unconditional love, 171
understanding, 105, 113, 147
unhappiness, 143, 145, 157
United States
  chemicals used in large amounts in, 58
  health care system, 4, 83, 84
  leading causes of death, 83, 85
  public water supply, 16
  ranking of health care indicators, 84, 85, 86
unity of life, 79, 87–88
University of London, 29, 90, 136, 158
University of Southern California, 39
US Congressional Subcommittee on Natural Agricultural Resources and Environment, 36
US Congressional Subcommittee on Oversight and Investigations, 35
US Environmental Protection Agency (EPA), 12, 35, 36, 37, 58, 63, 67, 68, 69, 70
USA Today, 31, 193

V
vanity, 122, 132, 142
vegetables, 21
vegetarianism, 6, 183
vibration, law of, 157–158, 173

vibration, principle of, 186
Vibrational Medicine (Gerber), 126, 193
vibration(s)
  effects on consciousness of, 95, 126, 133, 134, 146, 184
  effects on health of, 78, 95, 184
  electromagnetic vibrations, 110
  and emotions, 131
  energy as result of, 108, 113, 115
  exposure to, 109
  of God, 132
  graphic representation of, 160
  and harmony, 110, 113
  law of cycles and, 152
  light as, 119, 123
  and molecular imprinting, 111
  in music, 146
  nature of, 95–96
  and polarity, 121
  qualities of, 113, 121
  shifting to positive, 122, 132, 134, 153, 155, 156
  and spiritual laws, 127
  as studied by Clark, 67
  and thoughts, 121, 122, 126, 131, 132, 136
  and trigonometry, 184
vibratory energy, 33, 95, 111, 113, 115, 157
vibratory radiation, 33, 95, 160
video display terminals (VRTs), 37
viewpoints, changes of, 1, 130, 147
Virginia, environmental toxicants in, 59
viruses, 7, 21, 27, 38, 45, 96, 110, 112, 161, 169
vitamins, 19, 97, 165
vril, 92

VRTs (video display terminals), 37